Physical Characteristics of the Labrador Retriever

(from the American Kennel Club standard)

Topline: The back is strong and the topline is level from the withers to the croup when standing or moving. However, the loin should show evidence of flexibility for athletic endeavor.

Body: Short-coupled, with good spring of ribs tapering to a moderately wide chest. The underline is almost straight, with little or no tuck-up in mature animals. When viewed from the side, the Labrador Retriever shows a well-developed, but not exaggerated forechest.

Tail: Very thick at the base, gradually tapering toward the tip, of medium length, and extending no longer than to the hock having that peculiar rounded appearance that has been described as the "otter" tail.

Hindquarters: Broad, muscular and well-developed from the hip to the hock with well-turned stifles and strong short hocks. Viewed from the side, the angulation of the rear legs is in balance with the front.

Color: Coat colors are black, yellow and chocolate. Blacks are all black.

Size: The height at the withers for a dog is 22 to 24 inches; for a bitch is 21 to 23 inches. Approximate weight of dogs and bitches in working condition: dogs 65 to 80 pounds; bitches 55 to 70 pounds.

Feet: Strong and compact, with well-arched toes and well-developed pads. Dew claws may be removed.

Labrador Retriever

by Margaret A. Gilbert

9   **History of the** Labrador Retriever

Surely you know the Lab, but do you know his background? Learn about the first breeders and early ancestors on the isle of Newfoundland; follow the breed's travels to the U.K., where his hunting abilities were further developed; and welcome the Lab to the U.S.A., where he gained a stronghold and progressed to become America's favorite breed.

21   **Characteristics of the** Labrador Retriever

What's not to love about a Labrador? Friendly, even temperament, outgoing nature, trainability, versatility, loyalty, affection...and the list goes on! Study the breed's personality in detail, consider the requirements of owning a Lab and acquaint yourself with potential health concerns to see if you're the ideal owner for what many think of as the "ideal" dog.

28   **Breed Standard for the** Labrador Retriever

Learn the requirements of a well-bred Labrador Retriever by studying the description of the breed as set forth in the American Kennel Club's breed standard. Both show dogs and pets must possess key characteristics as outlined in the breed standard.

35   **Your Puppy** Labrador Retriever

Be advised about choosing a reputable breeder and selecting a healthy, typical puppy. Understand the responsibilities of ownership, including home preparation, acclimatization, the vet and prevention of common puppy problems.

63   **Everyday Care of Your** Labrador Retriever

Enter into a sensible discussion of dietary and feeding considerations, exercise, grooming, traveling and identification of your dog. This chapter discusses Labrador Retriever care for all stages of development.

78   **Training Your** Labrador Retriever

By Charlotte Schwartz
Be informed about the importance of training your Labrador Retriever from the basics of house-training and understanding the development of a young dog to executing obedience commands (sit, stay, down, etc.).

Contents

KENNEL CLUB BOOKS® LABRADOR RETRIEVER

ISBN 13: 978-1-59378-204-7

Copyright © 2003, **2008** • Kennel Club Books® • A Division of BowTie, Inc.
40 Broad Street, Freehold, NJ 07728 USA
Cover Design Patented: US 6,435,559 B2 • Printed in South Korea

Photography by Isabelle Français and Carol Ann Johnson with additional photographs by:

Norvia Behling, T. J. Calhoun, Carolina Biological Supply, David Dalton, Doskocil, James Hayden-Yoav, James R. Hayden, RBP, Lynette Hodge, Bill Jonas, Dwight R. Kuhn, Dr. Dennis Kunkel, Mikki Pet Products, Phototake, Jean Claude Revy, Dr. Andrew Spielman and Alice van Kempen.

Illustrations by Renée Low.

The publisher would like to thank all of the owners of the dogs featured in this book.

A sporting dog by trade, the Labrador Retriever has always been at home in the field. Today, the breed is equally at home...at home! The Lab is known the world over as a favorite family friend.

HISTORY OF THE
LABRADOR RETRIEVER

What introduction does the world's most popular dog require? Everyone has seen a Labrador Retriever romping happily with his family. Regarded as the ideal family dog for generations, the Labrador is by definition biddable and adaptable to practically any lifestyle.

It's common today to hear the breed simply referred to as the Labrador; however, this is by and large incorrect. The Labrador is a *retriever*. The Labrador Retriever, a prominent member of the AKC's Sporting Group, is a hunting dog by trade. The pet Labrador Retriever comes from a lineage of hard-working hunters who could spend tireless hours on upland game birds on rigorous terrain. While your pet Labrador Retriever may only fetch your slippers and the Sunday paper, it is helpful to understand that his predecessors pursued pheasant, duck and other wild fowl.

Well, that's the "retriever" part of his name; what's the meaning of the "Labrador" part? To truly understand the breed's origins, we must look not to Labrador, but to

In wood or water, the Labrador is a skilled and dependable hunting companion and retriever.

The Labrador Retriever's "soft mouth" makes him ideal for returning felled game undamaged.

the island off its southern shores called Newfoundland. The rich history of this island, originally inhabited by the Dorset Eskimos, dates back to the 1400s; however, it wasn't until the 1600s that the island became the home of wayward fishermen. These fishermen, it is believed, swam to the island after abandoning ships that were passing by the island. As these fishermen tended to be "free spirits" (like many today!), the island went without laws or establishments of any kind for the next two centuries, despite the inhabitation of these men.

The first dogs on the island of Newfoundland are traced to these fishermen, as there is no evidence of the Eskimos' having dogs on the island, and no dogs existed on Newfoundland when the fishermen landed there. As the Labrador Retriever was once called the Lesser Newfoundland Dog, it has often been presumed that the breed is related to the Newfoundland breed. The Newfoundland, well known to

dog lovers today, is a much larger, more abundantly coated, heavy-boned dog, showing much influence of its mastiff origins. Still, both the Newfoundland and the Labrador Retriever share the unique physical characteristic of webbed feet.

The terrain and weather conditions of Newfoundland are rugged, requiring a dog of surefootedness, stamina and "buoyancy." The size of the Labrador Retriever mattered tremendously, since the dog's had to fit into the fishermen's dories. The dogs' webbed feet speak well for the Labrador's ability to swim, even in the icy, rough waters of the North Atlantic. Among the other characteristics of our modern Labrador that "make sense" for a dog surviving on Newfoundland's brutal shores is the thick and waterproof coat. Another important feature of the breed is its broad chest, necessary for "surfing" against the strong waves and current of the unrelenting

The original Labrador Retrievers found in Newfoundland were predominately black, and today this is still the most numerous color in the breed.

While Labrador Retrievers have been useful for many tasks throughout their noble history, they have always been and still are treasured as trustworthy family pets.

North Atlantic. Since the island was bountiful in game, the fishermen were able to use their dogs to supplement their food supply from the land as well as from the sea.

The Newfoundlanders were importing quality retriever stock from England, though there was considerable variation in type. At this time (circa 1780–1810) any retriever—long-haired, curly-coated, short-coated, wavy-coated—was bred to produce other retrievers of excellent working ability. The division of the retriever breeds did not come until much later.

Labradors weren't the only dogs on the island at this point, as settlers brought other types; however, as the reputation of the Labrador grew, these other types were often replaced with Labradors. Since the Labrador's disposition and adaptability were so highly respected, hunters and sportsmen deemed them the dogs of choice. The retrievers soon replaced the pointers and setters that had stood beside these sportsmen. Although the Labrador Retriever that we know today comes in three acceptable colors, black, yellow and chocolate, the dogs on Newfoundland were principally black. These small black dogs were sometimes referred to as St. John's Water Dogs, and were called "the best of any kind of dog for shooting…by far."

A frustrating fact to breed enthusiasts today is that the residents of Newfoundland kept no records of the dogs on which they relied upon so heavily. Survival on this barren island was such an all-encompassing pursuit that there was little time for such record-keeping.

DEVELOPING POTENTIAL

The behavior and personality of your Labrador Retriever will reflect your care and training more than any breed characteristics or indications. Remember that these dogs require a purposeful existence, so plan your relationship around activities that serve this most basic and important need. All of the good potential of the breed will naturally follow.

THE LABRADOR COMES TO BRITAIN

The Second and Third Earls of Malmsbury are credited for exporting the famous St. John's Dogs from Newfoundland to Great Britain. The dogs at this point in time (around 1825) were sometimes called Little Newfoundlers. The Third Earl, the pioneer breeder of these dogs, is credited for changing the breed's name to Labrador Retriever. These gentry and others like them kept the Labradors pure, breeding them only to dogs imported from Newfoundland, as they were exceptional in their swimming, retrieving and fighting abilities. It is also said that any of the puppies from these St. John's Dogs that were crossed to other dogs usually maintained the strong appearance of the Labrador—black, short fur, a non-curling tail and webbed feet. As early as the 1870s, the "breed" was described as symmetrical and elegant, and the temperament was praised and considered a requirement for the utility of the Labrador. It's no doubt that the early breeders' commitment to a sound disposition in the Labrador contributed to the breed's forthcoming enormous popularity as a family dog around the world.

In 1903, the Labrador Retriever was recognized by England's Kennel Club. Later that year, the breed was listed separately as a member of the Gundog Group.

The Third Earl of Malmsbury established the name Labrador Retriever for the breed. The Labs shown represent each of the three colors—yellow, black and chocolate.

The retrievers at this point were still not divided by "breed" as we know them today. It was not until early 1905, when the Labrador Retriever was separately listed, that The Kennel Club began to differentiate between retriever "breeds." There is confusion in the records from these early days because some dogs were called "golden" and others "Labrador," though there is no indication about coat length. Thus, the "golden retrievers" may have indeed been yellow Labrador Retrievers. This was the early days of purebred dog enthusiasm. It must be stated that today many people in the general public do not know the difference between a yellow Labrador and the Golden Retriever (despite the long, wavy, luxurious coat of the latter). As a rule, we never call a yellow Labrador a "golden" Labrador.

The Kennel Club's stud books contain references to liver-colored wavy-coated retrievers. These dogs in actuality trace back to the chocolate Labrador Retrievers of the famous Buccleuch Kennels, the breeders responsible for six of the first seven retrievers entered in the stud book. Buccleuch Kennels produced the famous field trial champion by the name of Peter of Faskally, who is known to be behind many of the top Labradors from the early days as well as many of the top field dogs in England and the U.S.

In 1904, the Labrador Retriever was classified as a member of the Gundog Group by The Kennel Club. The breed is classified in the AKC's Sporting Group.

While black is considered the "original" color in the breed, yellow Labs steadily gained popularity throughout the 20th century.

Many of the early breed books still in print depict these famous dual champions.

The best yellow Labrador Retrievers are traced back to a dog by the name of Ben of Hyde, who was whelped in 1899. He was bred to many excellent black bitches, and his genes are buttoned on the top yellow Lab kennels throughout England. While the blacks have always dominated the other two colors, numerically, the period after World War II marked an increase in the yellow Labs' popularity.

Lorna, Countess Howe, along with Lord Knutsford, founded the U.K.'s Labrador Club in 1916 and held the first field trial there in 1920. Lord Knutsford authored the first Labrador Retriever breed standard in 1923, which is a written description of the ideal specimen of the breed. Knutsford's standard has changed very little to the present day. Countess Howe, considered the greatest of Labrador breeders, produced a number of dual champions—that is, dogs titled as both a bench (show) champion and a field trial champion. Not the least of Countess Howe's great Labradors was the first dual champion of the breed, Dual Ch. Banchory Bolo, the son of her very first Labrador, Scandal. It was Bolo with whom Countess Howe was most enamored, the dog who made her truly "head over hocks" for the Labrador Retriever breed.

BRAIN AND BRAWN

Since dogs have been inbred for centuries, their physical and mental characteristics are constantly being changed to suit man's desires for hunting, retrieving, scenting, guarding and warming their masters' laps. During the past 150 years, dogs have been judged according to physical characteristics as well as functional abilities. Few breeds can boast a genuine balance between physique, working ability and temperament.

England's Royal Family has long been associated with the Labrador. King George VI and Queen Elizabeth promoted Labradors at shows through their kennel known as Wolverton (more recently changed to Sandringham). The King entered dogs in the Crufts show, the U.K.'s largest show, in the 1920s and 1930s. The Queen actually entered field trials with her dogs—this illustrates the kinds of people attracted to field trials in England! George was the Patron of the Labrador Club, and was replaced by Elizabeth as Patroness after his death. Today in England, field trials are still supported by the Royal Family, and the annual championship is held at the Queen's shooting estate, Sandringham, in East Anglia. She is often in attendance at the British Retriever Championship in December each year.

The British shooting dogs, or working gundogs, are athletic in type and appearance. In order for a dog to excel in a field trial, it must possess discipline, control and responsiveness. It is much more difficult for a dog to achieve a field trial championship in Britain than it is in the U.S., where field trials are simulations of hunting situations. In the U.K., where the shooting sport originated, a field trial is an actual hunting episode, including wild birds and whatever else Mother Nature supplies. What makes hunting exciting is the surprise, and that element is essential to a field trial as well.

NEXT STOP: THE UNITED STATES

America extends its gratitude to Lorna, Countess Howe for exporting the first Labradors "back" to North America. Lest we forget, the Labrador began on Canadian shores! Sportsmen in Long Island, New York, were gifted by Countess Howe with the first Labradors to be seen in the U.S. This occurred shortly after World War I. Of course, the landscape of Long Island paints the perfect setting for a working Labrador Retriever, with its abundance of waterfowl, rolling oceanfront and range of temperatures.

To say that the Labrador Retriever caught on immediately

would not be true. Although the breed was first registered with the American Kennel Club in 1917, ten years later there were scarcely two dozen retrievers (of all types!) in the U.S. In fact, Labradors were classified under the broad heading of "Retrievers" until the late 1920s when distinctions were made between the different breeds. The first Labrador registered was a bitch of Scottish origin by the name of Brocklehirst Floss (AKC #223339). The breed was officially recognized in 1932.

While today Labs are kept by all types of American families, this was not originally the case. Instead, the upper-class wealthy families were attracted to shooting sports, popular in Scotland in the 1920s. These families brought game-keepers from Scotland onto their estates and imported Labradors from the finest English kennels, virtually converting their estates into shooting preserves, chock full of ducks and pheasants. It's important to note that these Labradors were imported for one purpose only—not to become beloved family pets or show dogs, but "to retrieve upland game and waterfowl." These same gentlefolk are responsible for the rise of field trials in America and thus the birth of the Labrador Retriever Club in 1931 in New York.

Franklin B. Lord, one of the club's founding members, held the club's first field trial in December 1931. A total of 27 dogs competed under two judges on a 8,000-acre estate. The club's first specialty

Lorna, Countess Howe sent the first Labrador Retrievers to the U.S.A. after World War I. The breed eventually progressed to become America's "top dog."

show occurred some 18 months later in 1933, attracting 33 dogs. The winner of the first specialty show was owned by Mr. Lord, a dog by the name of Boli of Blake, bred by Countess Howe. Boli also became the first bench champion of the breed.

Despite the interest in the breed that occurred between World War I and World War II, both wars had a deleterious effect on the Labrador and its numbers; this was the case with most dog breeds. It wasn't until after World War II that the Labrador Retriever gained a strong foothold in the United States. Imports from top British kennels, notably Sandy-lands kennel, re-energized the breed in the U.S. and these imported dogs had much influence on American conformation lines. Top British dogs and their descendants also appear in the pedigrees of many American field lines.

The trend toward two types of Labrador, those for show and those for the field, is not seen as beneficial to the breed by the national parent club, the Labrador Retriever Club, Inc. The club feels that all Labradors should be of the same type and should be able to perform the breed's intended functions, whether or not they are destined for the field, and that this should be the first criteria when judging Labs in the show ring. It does no service to the breed to have conformation winners that are not true Labradors with working type and ability! Therefore, the club defends the standard of the breed and sets the trend for the "correct" Labrador in the U.S.

The dissension in the Labrador Retriever breed in America is deep-rooted, and there is much variation in breed type as an unfortunate result. The height disqualification in the revised AKC standard renders most show dogs too short to enter the ring; nonetheless, dogs of incorrect height are seen all too frequently at shows. The Labrador Retriever Club, Inc. seeks to breed and

KEY CHARACTERISTICS

Bred to be a sporting dog, the Labrador must be well balanced and strongly built in order to perform his intended function. Breed standards differ from country to country; for example, the AKC standard's height range is 2 inches higher than that of the Kennel Club's. Problems lie not in small variation, but in gross exaggeration. The breed's overwhelming popularity and constant demand for puppies have made the Labrador vulnerable to irresponsible breeders who seem to think that bigger is better. Beware of purchasing a pup from oversized parents, as oversize leads to physical defects. Even though a Labrador does not reach full size until about two-and-a-half years of age, balance and good proportion are still evident in the young Lab. A balanced pup should grow into a balanced adult.

As stated in the AKC standard, "kind friendly eyes, imparting good temperment, intelligence and alertness are a hallmark of the breed"—and this picture says it all!

promote true-to-type dogs, tall enough to do the work and not nearly as heavy-set as most dogs that win in the show ring. The show ring enthusiasts claim that their dogs are not as high-strung as the hunting strains, though there is no doubt that the show dogs are not suited to last a whole day in the field retrieving game and waterfowl.

Despite this controversy, the Labrador Retriever, in all colors, shapes and sizes, reigns as America's number-one dog. It outregisters every other breed annually and has been on the top of the list for a decade! As a family pet, it is the dog of choice. Whether or not the 100,000-plus Labradors registered every year with the AKC can hunt, swim and retrieve to endure a day in the field seems immaterial to the millions of lovers of the pet Labrador. The breed's temperament and reliability, two qualities sought out by the early breeders, make it a flawless companion for dog folk of all ages.

Breed clubs work to ensure that the Labrador's original, essential characteristics are preserved through the generations in all dogs—working, pet or show.

CHARACTERISTICS OF THE
LABRADOR RETRIEVER

The answer to the question "Why the Labrador Retriever?" too often seems to be "Why not!" Since there are literally millions of happy Labrador lovers around the world, why shouldn't everyone love a Lab? Given the breed's good looks, trainability, loyalty, intelligence, etc., why isn't this the dog for everyone on the planet who loves dogs?! Let's begin by listing the kinds of people who should *not* consider the ubiquitous Labrador for their lives. Then we will examine the Labrador Retriever's character and the kinds of people who are ideal owners for this talented fellow.

OWNERS BEWARE!

POTENTIAL OWNERS WHO ARE LOOKING FOR A LAP DOG

The Lab is no lap dog. Sure he'll want to "lap" and kiss you constantly, but he's too big to sit on your lap while you're reading or spending time in front of the television. Labradors like to be close to you, that's for sure, but 60 pounds (or more) of true love is too much for anyone's lap!

POTENTIAL OWNERS WHO DO NOT LIKE EXERCISE

Labradors love to romp and play, preferably with their trusted owners close by. Since the breed is designed for chasing birds in the swamp or swimming toward fallen ducks, Labs most definitely have "energy to spare." Since most pet Labrador owners do not have the time or inclination to take their dogs out on weekend duck hunts, Labradors will need other outlets for their abundant energy.

SERVICE DOGS

The Labrador Retriever has been used in more areas of service to humankind than any other breed. Here are ten important areas that the breed has served:
1. Companions for all.
2. Hunting and retrieving for sportsmen.
3. Guides for the blind.
4. Hearing dogs for the deaf.
5. Arson and bomb detection.
6. Drug and substance detection.
7. Watch dogs for businesses and residences.
8. Search and rescue/avalanche and earthquake work.
9. Therapy dogs for hospitals.
10. Cancer detection.

Although known for their outdoor hunting pursuits, Labs are by no means outdoor-only dogs. They love to be indoors spending time with their loved ones.

POTENTIAL OWNERS WHO DO NOT HAVE A FENCED YARD

The Labrador needs a sizeable piece of property on which to exercise, and a fence is imperative. As a gundog, the Labrador does not have a strong sense of territory, and he will not guard his property the way a Rottweiler or Doberman Pinscher will. This is not to say that he is not protective—he is most protective of his family and home. However, if not fenced in he will more likely tear off in pursuit of a flapping pigeon than stay close by and stand watch.

POTENTIAL OWNERS WHO ARE SEEKING AN "ORNAMENTAL" OR OUTDOOR-ONLY DOG

The Labrador Retriever, for all his natural good looks and charm, does not fancy an owner that doesn't want to get up close to him and spend time with him indoors and out. Like most of the sporting breeds, the Labrador likes to be near his family inside the home. While it is true that the Labrador's ancestors were "kennel dogs," today's Labrador is strongly inclined to be indoors with his master and loved ones. To keep a Labrador outdoors exclusively will be torture to the poor dog, and such owners should consider a different breed or no dog at all. While the breed is renowned for its adaptability with any lifestyle, the breed is

It's no wonder that people love Labs! These friendly, trainable dogs are personable and loyal canine companions.

best when kept indoors and given time to spend outdoors. A happy Labrador is the true Labrador, and close to you is where your Labrador will want to be.

POTENTIAL OWNERS WHO ARE FUSSY ABOUT THEIR HOME

The Labrador sheds. Even though the breed has a short, dense coat, he does not cast coat any less than any other dog. Furthermore, the Labrador is not, as a rule, a genteel or docile animal—he's a "doggy" dog, and he likes to play inside and out. Owners will have to enforce the house rules immediately with the puppy, or else he may think he can roughhouse inside the house and out. Labradors can be raucous,

LOVE OF WATER

A dog with webbed feet must love to swim! Prized for their water retrieving abilities, Labradors naturally take to water and there's not many a Lab who will turn down the opportunity to get his paws wet. Pet Lab owners often enjoy runs and games of fetch on the beach with their dogs.

breed character further to better understand what kind of a dog the Labrador Retriever really is.

For all the talents of Labrador Retrievers, always top competitors in the nation's field trials and obedience trials, the breed is still only "canine." That is to say, the Labrador is not a "superdog." Mary Feazell, a Labrador fancier and trainer, contends that the 95 percent of what a Labrador can grow up to be depends upon the owner; only 5 percent depends on the dog itself. Such a huge responsibility for the owner of this fabulously talented dog! There is little that a Labrador cannot learn. Some Labradors recognize hundreds of words and can

rambunctious and rowdy—that's three "R's" potential owners may have to live with.

ARE YOU A LABRADOR PERSON?

If you have breezed through the first part of this chapter, thinking you are a good candidate for a Labrador, then let's explore the

Puppies will be puppies—and Labrador youngsters are among the most inquisitive and "on the go" pups of all breeds.

A world of potential lies within the Labrador, and it's up to the owner to develop it to the fullest.

execute dozens of commands. Feazell says, "Being realistic, Labs swim well, but they can't walk on water."

A Labrador Retriever requires a dedicated owner, whether the pursuit is basic obedience (such as sit, stay, come, etc., the commands necessary for a well-trained home companion) or more lofty pursuits like obedience trials, field trials, agility trials, working trials, etc. Many Labrador Retrievers are so intelligent and have such a strong desire to please that they become "self-trained." Labradors are excellent problem-solvers and quickly decide what pleases their masters and what does not! Such self-learned abilities include coming when called, staying where he's put, not bolting through the front door every time it is opened, not jumping up on visitors, permitting people to pet and touch him, not messing in the house, etc. Do not misunderstand. Labradors are smart, but you must be there to show the dog right from wrong. This is no different from instructing a child. Parents must be present for their children if they are to mature properly. Absent parents do not discipline, teach or help their children. Likewise, Labradors must receive enough training to make them capable of self-control and amenable to obeying commands, and minding their owners' wishes.

The owner controls what kind of dog his Labrador becomes. The owner provides the dog with training, guidance, encouragement and outlets for his energy and industry. The Labrador who

Despite its many joys, owning any puppy—even one as cute as a Labrador—is never always a "day at the beach."

Labs are affectionate dogs that love to be near their "people" and need to be a part of family life inside the home.

doesn't have proper "parental guidance" can develop behavioral problems, including destructive habits, aggression and fear-biting, to name a few. The owner molds his Labrador into the dog with whom he wants to live. Investing time, money and love into a dog can pay off a thousand-fold; skimping on the time and education that a dog as active and bright as a Labrador requires can be an owner's worst mistake. Do not rush into the ownership of a Labrador. This is a breed that deserves a top-quality owner, and if you're not sure about the acquisition, delay your decision.

Read more about the breed, talk to breeders, owners and trainers, attend a dog show and meet people who commit their lives to their dogs, and then you'll be better prepared to take the dive into dog ownership.

For those of you who are certain that a Labrador Retriever is the dog with whom you want to share your life, this wonderful dog can become your world. Whether it's a pet companion dog, show dog or field and working dog you require, the Labrador Retriever can become all you want in a faithful canine friend.

The Lab's expression conveys a biddable dog of sound temperament, traits essential to a working dog.

THE AMERICAN KENNEL CLUB STANDARD FOR THE LABRADOR RETRIEVER

GENERAL APPEARANCE
The Labrador Retriever is a strongly built, medium-sized, short-coupled dog possessing a sound, athletic, well-balanced conformation that enables it to function as a retrieving gun dog; the substance and soundness to hunt waterfowl or upland game for long hours under difficult conditions; the character and quality to win in the show ring; and the temperament to be a family companion. Physical features and mental characteristics should denote a dog bred to perform as an efficient Retriever of game with a stable temperament suitable for a variety of pursuits beyond the hunting environment.

The most distinguishing characteristics of the Labrador Retriever are its short, dense, weather resistant coat; an "otter" tail; a clean-cut head with broad back skull and moderate stop; powerful jaws; and its "kind," friendly eyes, expressing character, intelligence and good temperament.

Above all, a Labrador Retriever must be well balanced, enabling it to move in the show ring or work in the field with little or no effort. The typical Labrador possesses style and quality without over refinement, and substance without lumber or cloddiness. The Labrador is bred primarily as a working gun dog; structure and soundness are of great importance.

SIZE, PROPORTION AND SUBSTANCE
Size—The height at the withers for a dog is 22 to 24 inches; for a bitch is 21 to 23 inches. Any variance greater than 1 inch above or below these heights is a disqualification.

Approximate weight of dogs and bitches in working condition: dogs 65 to 80 pounds; bitches 55 to 70 pounds.

The minimum height ranges set forth in the paragraph above shall not apply to dogs or bitches under twelve months of age.

Proportion—Short-coupled; length from the point of the shoulder to the point of the rump is equal to or slightly longer than the distance from the withers to the ground. Distance from the elbow to the ground should be equal to one half of the height at the withers. The brisket should extend to the elbows, but not perceptibly deeper. The body must be of sufficient length to permit a straight, free and efficient stride; but the dog should never appear low and long or tall and leggy in outline.

Substance—Substance and bone proportionate to the overall dog. Light, "weedy" individuals are definitely incorrect; equally objectionable are cloddy lumbering specimens. Labrador Retrievers shall be shown in working condition well-muscled and without excess fat.

HEAD

Skull—The skull should be wide; well developed but without exaggeration. The skull and foreface should be on parallel planes and of approximately equal length. There should be a moderate stop—the brow slightly pronounced so that the skull is not absolutely in a straight line with the nose. The brow ridges aid in defining the stop. The head should be clean-cut and free from fleshy cheeks; the bony structure of the skull chiseled beneath the eye with no prominence in the cheek. The skull may show some median line; the occipital bone is not conspicuous in mature dogs. Lips should not be squared off or pendulous, but fall away in a curve toward the throat. A wedge-shape head, or a head long and narrow in muzzle and back skull is incorrect as are massive, cheeky heads. The jaws are powerful and free from snippiness— the muzzle neither long and narrow nor short and stubby.

Nose—The nose should be wide and the nostrils well-developed. The nose should be black on black or yellow dogs,

Labs must be intelligent, keen obedient and sturdy, besides having balanced, strong bodies.

and brown on chocolates. Nose color fading to a lighter shade is not a fault. A thoroughly pink nose or one lacking in any pigment is a disqualification.

Teeth—The teeth should be strong and regular with a scissors bite; the lower teeth just behind, but touching the inner side of the upper incisors. A level bite is acceptable, but not desirable. Undershot, overshot, or mis-aligned teeth are serious faults. Full dentition is preferred. Missing molars or pre-molars are serious faults.

Ears—The ears should hang moderately close to the head, set rather far back, and somewhat low on the skull; slightly above eye level. Ears should not be large and heavy, but in proportion with the skull and reach to the inside of the eye when pulled forward.

Eyes—Kind, friendly eyes imparting good temperament, intelligence and alertness are a hallmark of the breed. They should be of medium size, set well apart, and neither protruding nor deep set. Eye color should be brown in black and yellow Labradors, and brown or hazel in chocolates. Black, or yellow eyes give a harsh expression and are undesirable. Small eyes, set close together or round prominent eyes are not typical of the breed. Eye rims are black in black and yellow Labradors; and brown in chocolates. Eye rims without pigmentation is a disqualification.

NECK, TOPLINE AND BODY

Neck—The neck should be of proper length to allow the dog to retrieve game easily. It should be muscular and free from throati-ness. The neck should rise strongly from the shoulders with a moderate arch. A short, thick neck or a "ewe" neck is incorrect.

Topline—The back is strong and the topline is level from the withers to the croup when standing or moving. However, the loin should show evidence of flexibility for athletic endeavor.

Body—The Labrador should be short-coupled, with good spring of

The Labrador should have a moderately wide, well developed, but never exagger-ated, chest.

ribs tapering to a moderately wide chest. The Labrador should not be narrow chested; giving the appearance of hollowness between the front legs, nor should it have a wide spreading, bulldog-like front. Correct chest conformation will result in tapering between the front legs that allows unrestricted forelimb movement. Chest breadth that is either too wide or too narrow for efficient movement and stamina is incorrect. Slab-sided individuals are not typical of the breed; equally objectionable are rotund or barrel chested specimens. The underline is almost straight, with little or no tuck-up in mature animals. Loins should be short, wide and strong; extending to well developed, powerful hindquarters. When viewed from the side, the Labrador Retriever shows a well-developed, but not exaggerated forechest.

Tail—The tail is a distinguishing feature of the breed. It should be very thick at the base, gradually tapering toward the tip, of medium length, and extending no longer than to the hock. The tail should be free from feathering and clothed thickly all around with the Labrador's short, dense coat, thus having that peculiar rounded appearance that has been described as the "otter" tail. The tail should follow the topline in repose or when in motion. It may be carried gaily, but should not curl over the

back. Extremely short tails or long thin tails are serious faults. The tail completes the balance of the Labrador by giving it a flowing line from the top of the head to the tip of the tail. Docking or otherwise altering the length or natural carriage of the tail is a disqualification.

FOREQUARTERS

Forequarters should be muscular, well coordinated and balanced with the hindquarters.

Shoulders—The shoulders are well laid-back, long and sloping, forming an angle with the upper arm of approximately 90 degrees that permits the dog to move his forelegs in an easy manner with strong forward reach. Ideally, the length of the shoulder blade should equal the length of the upper arm. Straight shoulder blades, short upper arms or heavily muscled or loaded shoulders, all restricting free movement, are incorrect.

Front Legs—When viewed from the front, the legs should be straight with good strong bone. Too much bone is as undesirable as too little bone, and short legged, heavy boned individuals are not typical of the breed. Viewed from the side, the elbows should be directly under the withers, and the front legs should be perpendicular to the ground and well under the body. The elbows should be close to the

	CORRECT	**INCORRECT**

EARS
Set rather far back and hanging rather close to the head.

BITE
Teeth should be strong and regular in a scissor bite; jaw should not be undershot.

FOREQUARTERS
Forelegs should be straight with strong bone, not bowing out at the elbows.

FEET
Strong, compact, with well-arched toes; not hare-footed or splay-footed.

TAIL
The distinctive "otter" tail should appear rounded; may be carried gaily but never curling over back.

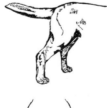 

HINDQUARTERS
Parallel when viewed from rear; cowhocks are highly undesirable.

ribs without looseness. Tied-in elbows or being "out at the elbows" interfere with free movement and are serious faults. Pasterns should be strong and short and should slope slightly from the perpendicular line of the leg. Feet are strong and compact, with well-arched toes and well-developed pads. Dew claws may be removed. Splayed feet, hare feet, knuckling over, or feet turning in or out are serious faults.

HINDQUARTERS

The Labrador's hindquarters are broad, muscular and well-developed from the hip to the hock with well-turned stifles and strong short hocks. Viewed from the rear, the hind legs are straight and parallel. Viewed from the side, the angulation of the rear legs is in balance with the front. The hind legs are strongly boned, muscled with moderate angulation at the stifle, and powerful, clearly defined thighs. The stifle is strong and there is no slippage of the patellae while in motion or when standing. The hock joints are strong, well let down and do not slip or hyper-extend while in motion or when standing. Angulation of both stifle and hock joint is such as to achieve the optimal balance of drive and traction. When standing the rear toes are only slightly behind the point of the rump. Over angula-

tion produces a sloping topline not typical of the breed. Feet are strong and compact, with well-arched toes and well-developed pads. Cow-hocks, spread hocks, sickle hocks and over-angulation are serious structural defects and are to be faulted.

COAT

The coat is a distinctive feature of the Labrador Retriever. It should be short, straight and very dense, giving a fairly hard feeling to the hand. The Labrador should have a soft, weather-resistant undercoat that provides protection from water, cold and all types of ground cover. A slight wave down the back is permissible. Woolly coats, soft silky coats, and sparse slick coats are not typical of the breed, and should be severely penalized.

COLOR

The Labrador Retriever coat colors are black, yellow and chocolate. Any other color or a combination of colors is a disqualification. A small white spot on the chest is permissible, but not desirable. White hairs from aging or scarring are not to be misinterpreted as brindling.

Black—Blacks are all black. A black with brindle markings or a black with tan markings is a disqualification.

Yellow—Yellows may range in color from fox-red to light cream,

Correct movement indicates correct body structure; show judges evaluate the dog's gait in the ring.

viewing the dog from the rear, one should have the impression that the hind legs move as nearly as possible in a parallel line with the front legs. The hocks should do their full share of the work, flexing well, giving the appearance of power and strength. When viewed from the side, the shoulders should move freely and effortlessly, and the foreleg should reach forward close to the ground with extension. A short, choppy movement or high knee action indicates a straight shoulder; paddling indicates long, weak pasterns; and a short, stilted rear gait indicates a straight rear assembly; all are serious faults. Movement faults interfering with performance including weaving; side-winding; crossing over; high knee action; paddling; and short, choppy movement, should be severely penalized.

with variations in shading on the ears, back, and underparts of the dog.

Chocolate—Chocolates can vary in shade from light to dark chocolate. Chocolate with brindle or tan markings is a disqualification.

MOVEMENT

Movement of the Labrador Retriever should be free and effortless. When watching a dog move toward oneself, there should be no sign of elbows out. Rather, the elbows should be held neatly to the body with the legs not too close together. Moving straight forward without pacing or weaving, the legs should form straight lines, with all parts moving in the same plane. Upon

TEMPERAMENT

True Labrador Retriever temperament is as much a hallmark of the breed as the "otter" tail. The ideal disposition is one of a kindly, outgoing, tractable nature; eager to please and non-aggressive towards man or animal. The Labrador has much that appeals to people; his gentle ways, intelligence and adaptability make him an ideal dog. Aggressiveness towards humans or other animals, or any evidence of shyness in an adult should be severely penalized.

LABRADOR RETRIEVER

OWNER CONSIDERATIONS

A purebred dog as versatile and talented as the Labrador Retriever attracts many admirers. Whether you are seeking a puppy simply as a home companion and family pet, as a show dog, as a field dog or as a competition dog, there are many serious factors governing your choice. You believe that you have enough time to devote to your new Labrador. Even a pet Labrador will require considerable time to train. Naturally, a field dog or obedience/agility dog will require hours of daily attention and special training. Do not take the acquisition of a Labrador Retriever lightly. This is a demanding dog who will want to share his whole life with you. The Labrador Retriever usually lives ten to fourteen years, which is a considerable portion of your human life. Do you know where you will be in a decade? You have to plan for your Labrador Retriever to be a part of that picture.

Consider the exercise that a dog as active as the Labrador will require. You have a fenced yard, so there is no worry that your curious pup will not go wandering down the lane to find your neighbors and their dogs, cats and horses! If you are not committed to the welfare and whole existence of this energetic, purposeful animal; if, in the simplest, most basic example, you

PUPPY APPEARANCE

Your puppy should have a well-fed appearance but not a distended abdomen, which may indicate worms or incorrect feeding, or both. The body should be firm, with a solid feel. The skin of the abdomen should be pale pink and clean, without signs of scratching or rash. Check to see if the dewclaws have been removed, as this is usually done when pups are very young.

One look at the Lab puppy's face and you'll surely be charmed—but be sure to use your head in making your decision.

restrictions to your freedom (of movement), as in vacations or weekend trips. This union is a serious affair and should be deeply considered, but, once decided, your choice of a Labrador Retriever is, perhaps, the most rewarding of all breeds. A few suggestions will help in the purchase of your dog.

ACQUIRING A PUPPY
The safest method of obtaining your puppy is to seek out a

are not willing to walk your dog daily, despite the weather, do not choose a Labrador Retriever as a companion.

Space is another important consideration. The Labrador Retriever in early puppyhood may be well accommodated in a corner of your kitchen but, after only six months, when the dog is likely over 60 pounds, larger space certainly will be required. You will have to train your Labrador to understand the house rules so that you can trust him in every room of your house. Of course, puppy-proofing is vital.

Along with these factors, there are the usual problems associated with puppies of any breed, such as the damages likely to be sustained by your floors, furniture and flowers, and, not least of all,

PUPPY'S PAPERS
Too often new owners are confused about two of the important documents that they receive with their puppy—the pedigree and the registration. Your puppy's pedigree, essentially a family tree, is a written record of a dog's genealogy of three generations or more. The pedigree will show you the names as well as performance titles of all the dogs in your pup's background. Your breeder must provide you with a registration application, with his part properly filled out. You must complete the application and send it to the AKC with the proper fee. The seller must provide you with complete records to identify the puppy. The AKC requires that the seller provide the buyer with the following: breed; sex, color and markings; date of birth; litter number (when available); names and registration numbers of the parents; breeder's name; and date sold or delivered.

reputable breeder. This is suggested even if you are not looking for a show specimen or a top contender in field work. The novice breeders and pet owners who advertise at attractive prices in the local newspapers are probably kind enough toward their dogs, but perhaps do not have the expertise or facilities required to successfully raise these animals. A lack of proper feeding can cause indigestion, rickets, weak bones, poor teeth and other problems. Veterinary bills may soon distort initial savings into financial or worse, emotional loss.

Inquire about vaccinations and when the puppy was last dosed for worms. Check the ears. Ear-mite infestation is very common in young puppies. Left untreated, mite infestation can damage a pup's hearing. Keep on guard for the pup's scratching or shaking its head.

Color is a matter of personal choice, but whichever color you prefer, your puppy should have good pigmentation. In black Labradors, everything is black; in

Retrievers by nature, Labs of all ages tend to be orally fixated and will need plenty of safe chew toys.

chocolates, the dog's nose and paws should match his color. Yellows have black noses. The shades of yellows and chocolates can vary considerably, but avoid white markings, tan marks on chocolates and patches of brindle (combination of brown and black hairs). While no importance is placed on color in the breed, only the three colors—yellow, black and chocolate—are recognized as true Labradors.

Note the way your choice moves. The Labrador Retriever, even in puppyhood, should show light and swift movement with no tendency to stumble or drag the hind feet. Look at the mouth to make sure that the bite is fairly even, although maturity can often correct errors present at puppyhood. If you have any doubts, ask to see the parents' mouths. This brings up an important point—do not purchase

HEALTH FIRST
You should not even think about buying a puppy that looks sick, undernourished, overly frightened or nervous. Sometimes a timid puppy will warm up to you after a 30-minute "let's-get-acquainted" session.

Raising an energetic Lab pup to be a well-behaved adult is quite an endeavor, but one that will reward you greatly with a loyal canine companion and friend.

a puppy without first seeing at least one of the parents.

Male dogs of this breed are equally devoted and loyal but have the drawback of being in season all year and, therefore, prone to possible wandering. This is the central reason why females are always chosen as guide dogs for the blind. Of course, good breeders will require that pet puppies be neutered or spayed, thus eliminating problems related to sexual behavior.

Your home must be prepared for the arrival of your new explorer, and all of his expeditions should be supervised carefully.

COMMITMENT OF OWNERSHIP

After considering all of these factors, you have most likely already made some very important decisions about selecting your puppy. You have chosen a Labrador Retriever, which means that you have decided which characteristics you want in a dog and what type of dog will best fit into your family and lifestyle. If you have selected a breeder, you have gone a step further—you have done your research and found a responsible, conscientious person who breeds quality Labrador Retrievers and who should be a reliable source of help as you and your puppy adjust to life together. If you have observed a litter in action, you have obtained a firsthand look at the dynamics of a puppy "pack" and, thus, you have gotten to learn about each pup's individual personality—perhaps you have even found one that particularly appeals to you.

However, even if you have not yet found the Labrador Retriever puppy of your dreams, observing pups will help you learn to recognize certain behavior and to determine what a pup's behavior indicates about his temperament. You will be able to pick out which pups are the leaders, which ones are less outgoing, which ones are confident, which ones are shy, playful, friendly, aggressive, etc. Equally as important,

ARE YOU A FIT OWNER?

If the breeder from whom you are buying a puppy asks you a lot of personal questions, do not be insulted. Good breeders care deeply about each of their puppies futures, and such a breeder wants to be sure that you will be a fit provider for his puppy.

ARE YOU PREPARED?

Unfortunately, when a puppy is bought by someone who does not take into consideration the time and attention that dog ownership requires, it is the puppy who suffers when he is either abandoned or placed in a shelter by a frustrated owner. So all of the "homework" you do in preparation for your pup's arrival will benefit you both. The more informed you are, the more you will know what to expect and the better equipped you will be to handle the ups and downs of raising a puppy. Hopefully, everyone in the household is willing to do his part in raising and caring for the pup. The anticipation of owning a dog often brings a lot of promises from excited family members: "I will walk him every day," "I will feed him," "I will house-train him," etc., but these things take time and effort, and promises can easily be forgotten once the novelty of the new pet has worn off.

you will learn to recognize what a healthy pup should look and act like. All of these things will help you in your search, and when you find the Labrador Retriever that was meant for you, you will know it, and the feeling will be mutual.

Researching your breed, selecting a responsible breeder and observing as many pups as possible are all important steps on the way to dog ownership. It may seem like a lot of effort...and you have not even brought the pup home yet! Remember, though, you cannot be too careful when it comes to deciding on the type of dog you want and finding out about your prospective pup's background. Buying a puppy is not—or *should* not be—just another whimsical purchase. In fact, this is one instance in which you actually *do* get to choose your own family! But, you may be thinking, buying a puppy should be fun—it should not be so serious and so much work. If you keep in mind the thought that your puppy is not a cuddly stuffed toy or decorative lawn ornament, but instead will become a real member of your family, you will realize that while buying a puppy is a pleasurable and exciting endeavor, it is not something to be taken lightly. Relax...the fun will start when the pup comes home!

Always keep in mind that a puppy is nothing more than a

baby in a furry disguise…a baby who is virtually helpless in a human world and who trusts his owner for fulfillment of his basic needs for survival. That goes beyond food, water and shelter; your pup needs care, protection, guidance and love. If you are not prepared to commit to this, then you are not prepared to own a dog.

"Wait a minute," you say. "How hard could this be? All of my neighbors own dogs and they seem to be doing just fine. Why should I have to worry about all

of this?" Well, you should *not* worry about it; in fact, you will probably find that once your Labrador Retriever pup gets used to his new home, he will fall into his place in the family quite naturally. But it never hurts to emphasize the commitment of dog ownership. With some time and patience, it is really not too difficult to raise a curious and exuberant Labrador Retriever pup to be a well-adjusted and well-mannered adult dog—a dog that could be your most loyal friend.

A hungry, litter and a proud—and busy—mom.

PREPARING PUPPY'S PLACE IN YOUR HOME

Researching your breed and finding a breeder are only two aspects of the "homework" you will have to do before bringing your Labrador Retriever puppy home. You will also have to prepare your home and family for the new addition. Much like you would prepare a nursery for a newborn baby, you will need to designate a place in your home that will be the puppy's own. How you prepare your home will depend on how much freedom the dog will be allowed: will he be confined to a specific area in the house, or will he be allowed to roam as he pleases? Whatever you decide, you must ensure that he has a place that he can "call his own."

When you bring your new puppy into your home, you are bringing him into what will become his home as well. Obviously, you did not buy a puppy so that he could take control of your house, but in order for a puppy to grow into a stable, well-adjusted dog, he has to feel comfortable in his surroundings. Remember, he is leaving the warmth and security of his mother and littermates, plus the familiarity of the only place he has ever known, so it is important to make his transition as easy as possible. By preparing a place in your home for the puppy, you are making him feel as welcome as possible in a strange new place. It should not take him long to get used to it, but the sudden shock of being transplanted is somewhat

The fun part of your "homework" will be visiting Labrador litters and watching these small wonders in action.

It takes a skilled photographer to get a "still life" picture of Lab puppies!

traumatic for a young pup. Imagine how a small child would feel in the same situation—that is how your puppy must be feeling. It is up to you to reassure him and to let him know, "Little fellow, you are going to like it here!"

WHAT YOU SHOULD BUY

CRATE

To someone unfamiliar with the use of crates in dog training, it may seem like punishment to shut

PUPPY PROBLEMS

The majority of problems that are commonly seen in young pups will disappear as your Labrador Retriever gets older. However, how you deal with problems when he is young will determine how he reacts to discipline as an adult dog. It is important to establish who is boss (hopefully it will be you!) right away when you are first bonding with your Labrador Retriever. This bond will set the tone for the rest of your life together.

A crate-trained Lab will be amenable to safe confinement wherever you go, making life easier for all concerned.

A crate-trained Lab will be amenable to safe confinement wherever you go, making life easier for all concerned.

As far as purchasing a crate, the type that you buy is up to you. It will most likely be one of the two most popular types: wire or fiberglass. There are advantages and disadvantages to each type. For example, a wire crate is more open, allowing the air to flow

a dog in a crate; this is not the case at all. Crates are not cruel—crates have many humane and highly effective uses in dog care and training. For example, crate training is a very popular and very successful housebreaking method, a crate can keep your dog safe during travel and, perhaps most importantly, a crate provides your dog with a place of his own in your home. It serves as a "doggie bedroom" of sorts—your Labrador Retriever can curl up in his crate when he wants to sleep or when he just needs a break. Many dogs sleep in their crates overnight. With a soft blanket and his favorite toy, a crate becomes a cozy pseudo-den for your dog. Like his ancestors, he too will seek out the comfort and retreat of a den—you just happen to be providing him with something a little more luxurious than leaves and twigs lining a dirty ditch.

CRATE-TRAINING TIPS

During crate training, you should partition off the section of the crate in which the pup stays. If he is given too big an area, this will hinder your training efforts. Crate training is based on the fact that a dog does not like to soil his sleeping quarters, so it is ineffective to keep a pup in an area that is so big that he can eliminate in one end and get far enough away from it to sleep. Also, you want to make the crate den-like for the pup. Blankets and a favorite toy will make the crate cozy for the small pup; as he grows, you may want to evict some of his "roommates" to make more room. It will take some coaxing at first, but be patient. Given some time to get used to it, your pup will adapt to his new home-within-a-home quite nicely.

PHOTO COURTESY OF DOSKOCIL.

and the inclination to buy a new crate every time your pup has a growth spurt, it is better to get one that will accommodate your dog both as a pup and at full size. A large crate will be necessary for a full-grown Labrador Retriever, as the breed's approximate weight range is between 55 and 80 pounds.

BEDDING

A crate pad, soft bedding or a blanket in the dog's crate will help the dog feel more at home. First, this will take the place of the leaves, twigs, etc., that the pup would use in the wild to make a den; the pup can make his own "burrow" in the crate. Although your pup is far removed from his den-making ancestors, the denning instinct is still a part of his genetic makeup. Second, until you bring your pup home, he has been sleeping amid the warmth of his mother and litter-mates, and while a blanket is not the same as a warm, breathing body, it still provides heat and something with

Your local pet shop will offer many types and sizes of crates. Choose a sturdy crate for your Lab puppy that will comfortably house him as an adult.

through and affording the dog a view of what is going on around him. Wire crates are excellent for use in the home. A fiberglass crate, however, is sturdier and can double as a travel crate since it provides more protection for the dog.

The size of the crate is another thing to consider. Puppies do not stay puppies forever—in fact, sometimes it seems as if they grow right before your eyes. A small crate may be fine for a very young Labrador Retriever pup, but it will not do him much good for long! Unless you have the money

TEETHING TIP
Puppies like soft toys for chewing. Because they are teething, soft items like stuffed toys soothe their aching gums and give them some added relief.

which to snuggle. You will want to wash your pup's bedding frequently in case he has a potty accident in his crate, and replace or remove anything that becomes ragged and starts to fall apart.

Toys

Toys are a must for dogs of all ages, especially for curious playful pups. Puppies are the "children" of the dog world, and what child does not love toys? Chew toys provide enjoyment to both dog and owner—your dog will enjoy playing with his favorite toys, while you will enjoy the fact that they distract him from your expensive shoes and leather sofa. Puppies love to chew; in fact, chewing is a physical need for pups as they are teething, and everything looks appetizing! The full range of your possessions—from old dish rag to Oriental rug—are fair game in the eyes of a teething pup. Puppies are not all that discerning when it comes to

Blankets, pillows or just about anything soft and snugly will be appreciated by your Lab throughout his life.

finding something to literally "sink their teeth into"—everything tastes great!

Offer sturdy toys, like strong nylon bones and chew devices, to your Labrador Retriever. Get large-size toys for adult dogs. Stuffed toys are another option; these are good to put in the dog's crate to give him some company. Be careful of these, as a pup can de-stuff one pretty quickly, and stay away from stuffed toys with small plastic eyes or parts that a pup could choke on. Similarly, squeaky toys are quite popular. There are dogs that will come running from anywhere in the house at the first sound from their favorite squeaky friend. However, if a pup de-stuffs one of these, the small plastic squeaker inside can be dangerous if swallowed. Monitor the condition of your pup's toys carefully and get rid of any that have been chewed to the point of becoming potentially dangerous.

Be careful of natural bones, which have a tendency to splinter into sharp, dangerous pieces. Also be careful of rawhide, which after enough chewing can turn into pieces that are easy to swallow, and also watch out for the mushy mess it can turn into on your carpet.

Leash

A nylon leash is probably the best option, as it is the most resistant

Pet shops have a large selection of safe, durable pet toys suitable for training and entertaining your Lab.

to puppy teeth should your pup take a liking to chewing on his leash. Of course, this is a habit that should be nipped in the bud, but, if your pup likes to chew on his leash, he has a very slim chance of being able to chew through the strong nylon. Nylon leashes are also lightweight, which is good for a young Labrador Retriever who is just getting used to the idea of walking on a leash. For everyday walking and safety purposes, the nylon leash is a good choice.

As your pup grows up and gets used to walking on the leash, and can do it politely, you may want to purchase a flexible leash, which allows you either to extend the length to give the dog a broader area to explore or to pull in the leash when you want to keep him close. If your Labrador Retriever is especially strong or tends to pull on the leash, you may want to purchase something stronger, like a thick leather leash. Of course there are also special leashes for training purposes, and specially made harnesses for the working Labrador Retriever.

COLLAR

Your pup should get used to wearing a collar all the time since you will want to attach his ID tags to his collar. Also, the leash

Choke collars should only be used for training and require expertise on the part of the owner.

FOOD AND WATER BOWLS

Your pup will need two bowls, one for food and one for water. You may want two sets of bowls, one for inside and one for outside, depending on where the dog will be fed and where he will be spending time. Stainless steel or sturdy plastic bowls are popular choices. Although plastic bowls are more chewable, dogs tend not to chew on the steel variety, which can also be sterilized. It is very important thing is to buy sturdy bowls since, again, anything is in danger of being chewed by puppy teeth and you

and collar go hand in hand—you have to attach the leash to something! A lightweight nylon collar will be a good choice; make sure that it fits snugly enough so that the pup cannot wriggle out of it, but is loose enough so that it will not be uncomfortably tight around the pup's neck. You should be able to fit a finger in between the pup and the collar. It may take some time for your pup to get used to wearing the collar, but soon he will not even notice that it is there. Choke collars are made for training, but should only be used by an owner who knows exactly how to use it. If you use a stronger leather leash or a chain leash to walk your Labrador Retriever, you will need a stronger collar as well.

TOYS, TOYS, TOYS!

With a big variety of dog toys available, and so many that look like they would be a lot of fun for a dog, be careful in your selection. It is amazing what a set of puppy teeth can do to an innocent-looking toy; so, obviously, safety is a major consideration. Be sure to choose the most durable products that you can find. Hard nylon bones and toys are a safe bet, and many of them are offered in different scents and flavors that will be sure to capture your dog's attention. It is always fun to play a game of fetch with your dog, and there are balls and flying discs that are specially made to withstand dog teeth.

do not want your dog to be constantly chewing apart his bowl (for his safety and for your wallet!).

It is advised to put your Labrador's food and water bowls on elevated bowl stands; this brings the bowls closer to the dog's level so he does not have to crane his neck to reach, thus aiding his digestion and helping to guard against bloat or gastric torsion, a condition that affects deep-chested dogs like the Labrador.

CLEANING SUPPLIES

A pup that is not house-trained means you will be doing a lot of cleaning until he is. "Accidents" will occur, which is okay for now because the pup does not know any better. All you can do is clean up any accidents—old rags, paper towels, newspapers and a safe disinfectant are good to have on hand.

BEYOND THE BASICS

The items previously discussed are the bare necessities. You will find out what else you need as you go along—grooming supplies, flea/tick protection, baby gates to partition a room, etc. These things will vary depending on your situation. It is just important that right away you have everything you need to feed and make your Labrador Retriever comfortable in his first few days at home.

Purchase durable, easily cleaned bowls for your Lab. Consider buying two sets... one for inside and one for outside, plus stands on which to elevate the bowls.

Always be sure
your Lab has
clean water
available.

PUPPY-PROOFING YOUR HOME

Aside from making sure that your Labrador Retriever will be comfortable in your home, you also have to make sure that your home is safe for your Labrador Retriever. This means taking precautions to make sure that your pup will not get into anything he should not get into and that there is nothing within his reach that may harm him should he sniff it, chew it, inspect it, etc. This probably seems obvious since, while you are primarily concerned with your pup's safety, at the same time you do not want your belongings to be ruined.

Breakables should be placed out of reach if your dog is to have full run of the house. If he is to be limited to certain places within the house, keep any potentially dangerous items in the "off-limits" areas. An electrical cord can pose a danger should the puppy decide to taste it—and who is going to convince a pup that it would not make a great chew toy? Cords should be fastened tightly against the wall and kept from puppy's teeth. If your dog is going to spend time in a crate, make sure that there is nothing near his crate that he can reach if he sticks his curious little nose or paws through the openings. And just as you would with a child, keep all household cleaners and chemicals where the pup cannot get to them.

It is just as important to make sure that the outside of your home is safe. Of course, your puppy should never be unsupervised, but a pup let loose in the yard will want to run and explore, and he should be granted that freedom. Do not let a fence give you a false sense of security; you would be surprised how crafty (and persistent) a dog can be in figuring out how to dig under and squeeze his way through small holes, or to jump or climb over a fence. The

DOG OR BITCH?

Both the male and female Anatolian make excellent companions and are equally alert and protective. Their primary difference is in height and weigh,t and sometimes in abundance of coat, with males being greater in these respects. Young males can become especially assertive as they approach sexual maturity and require a firm hand so that bad habits are not established.

remedy is to make the fence high enough so that it really is impossible for your dog to get over it (about 6 feet should suffice), and well embedded into the ground. Be sure to repair or secure any gaps in the fence. Check the fence periodically to ensure that it is in good shape and make repairs as needed; a very determined pup may return to the same spot to "work on it" until he is able to get through.

FIRST TRIP TO THE VET
So, you have picked out your puppy and your home and family are ready. Now all you have to do

A black Lab and a young friend make themselves comfortable.

is pick your Labrador Retriever up from the breeder and the fun begins, right? Well...not so fast. Something else you need to prepare for is your pup's first trip to the veterinarian. Perhaps the breeder can recommend someone in the area who specializes in Labrador Retrievers, or the retriever breeds, or maybe you know some other Lab owners who can suggest a good vet. Either way, you should have an appointment arranged for your pup before you pick him up; plan on taking him for a check-up within the first few days of bringing him home.

The pup's first visit will consist of an overall examination to make sure that the pup does not have any problems that are not apparent to you. The veterinarian will also set up a schedule for the pup's vaccinations; the breeder will inform you of which ones the pup has already received and the vet can continue from there.

PET INSURANCE
Just like you can insure your car, your house and your own health, you likewise can insure your dog's health. Investigate a pet insurance policy by talking to your vet. Depending on the age of your dog, the breed and the kind of coverage you desire, your policy can be very affordable. Most policies cover accidental injuries, poisoning and thousands of medical problems and illnesses, including cancers. Some carriers also offer routine care and immunization coverage, including heartworm preventative, prescription flea control, annual check-ups, teeth cleaning, spaying/neutering, health screening and more. These policies are more costly than the others, but may be well worth the investment.

INTRODUCTION TO THE FAMILY

Everyone in the house will be excited about the puppy's coming home and will want to pet him and play with him, but it is best to make the introduction low-key so as not to overwhelm the puppy. He is apprehensive already; it is the first time he has been separated from his mother and the breeder, and the ride to your home is likely the first time he has been in a car. The last thing you want to do is smother him, as this will only frighten him further. This is not to say that human contact is not extremely necessary at this stage, because this is the time when an instant connection between the pup and his human family is formed. Gentle petting and soothing words should help console him, as well as just

SKULL & CROSSBONES

Thoroughly puppy-proof your house before bringing your puppy home. Never use cockroach or rodent poisons or plant fertilizers in any area accessible to the puppy. Avoid the use of toilet cleaners. Most dogs are born with "toilet-bowl sonar" and will take a drink if the lid is left open. Also keep the trash secured and out of the dog's reach.

putting him down and letting him explore on his own (under your watchful eye, of course).

The pup may approach family members or may busy himself with exploring for a while. Gradually, each person should spend some time with the pup, one at a time, crouching down to get as close to the pup's level as possible and letting him

"On the move" is a good descriptive term for Lab puppies—just look at this pack at play!

STRESS-FREE
Some experts in canine health advise that stress during a dog's early years of development can compromise and weaken his immune system, and may trigger the potential for a shortened life. They emphasize the need for happy and stress-free growing-up years.

YOUR PUP'S FIRST NIGHT HOME

You have traveled home with your new charge safely in his crate. He's been to the vet for a thorough check-up; he's been weighed, his papers examined; perhaps he's even been vaccinated and wormed as well. He's met the family and licked the whole family, including the excited children and the less-than-happy cat. He's explored his area, his new bed, the yard and anywhere else he's been permitted. He's eaten his first meal at home and relieved himself in the proper place. He's heard lots of new sounds, smelled new friends and seen more of the outside world than ever before.

That was the just the first day! He's exhausted and is ready for bed...or so you think!

It's puppy's first night and you are ready to say "Good night"— keep in mind that this is puppy's

The warmth and security of his littermates is what your pup will miss most when he leaves the breeder. Provide him with a cozy place to sleep and settle in.

sniff their hands and petting him gently. The puppy definitely needs human attention and needs to be touched—this is how to form an immediate bond. Just remember that the pup is experiencing a lot of things for the first time, all at the same time. There are new people, new noises, new smells and new things to investigate, so be gentle, be affectionate and be as comforting as you can be.

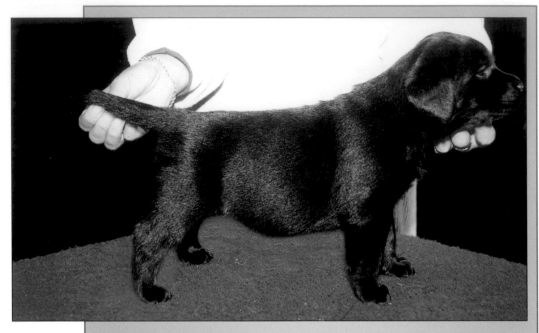

TEMPERAMENT COUNTS

Your selection of a good puppy can be determined by your needs. A show potential or a good pet? It is your choice. Every puppy, however, should be of good temperament. Although show-quality puppies are bred and raised with emphasis on physical conformation, responsible breeders strive for equally good temperament. Do not buy from a breeder who concentrates solely on physical beauty at the expense of personality.

first night ever to be sleeping alone. His dam and littermates are no longer at paw's length and he's a bit scared, cold and lonely. Be reassuring to your new family member. This is not the time to spoil him and give in to his inevitable whining.

Puppies whine. They whine to let others know where they are and hopefully to get company out of it. Place your pup in his new bed or crate in his room and close

the crate door. Mercifully, he will fall asleep without a peep. When the inevitable occurs, ignore the whining; he is fine. Be strong and keep his interest in mind. Do not allow your heart to become guilty and visit the pup. He will fall asleep.

Many breeders recommend placing a piece of bedding from the pup's former home in his new bed so that he recognizes the scent of his littermates. Others still advise placing a hot water bottle in his bed for warmth. This latter may be a good idea provided the pup doesn't attempt to suckle—he'll get good and wet and may not fall asleep so fast.

Puppy's first night can be somewhat stressful for the pup and his new family. Remember that you are setting the tone of nighttime at your house. Unless you want to play with your pup every night at 10 p.m., midnight

PUP MEETS WORLD

Thorough socialization includes not only meeting new people but also being introduced to new experiences such as riding in the car, having his coat brushed, hearing the television, walking in a crowd—the list is endless. The more your pup experiences, and the more positive the experiences are, the less of a shock and the less frightening it will be for your pup to encounter new things.

Like mother, like puppy! Young puppies receive important life lessons and essential early socialization during the time spent at the breeder's with their dam and littermates.

MANNERS MATTER

During the socialization process, a puppy should meet people, experience different environments and definitely be exposed to other canines. Through playing and interacting with other dogs, your puppy will learn lessons, ranging from controlling the pressure of his jaws by biting his littermates to the inner workings of the canine pack that he will apply to his human relationships for the rest of his life. That is why removing a puppy from its litter too early (before eight weeks) can be detrimental to the pup's development.

and 2 a.m., don't initiate the habit. Surely your family will thank you, and eventually so will your pup!

PREVENTING PUPPY PROBLEMS

SOCIALIZATION

Now that you have done all of the preparatory work and have helped your pup get accustomed to his new home and family, it is about time for you to have some fun! Socializing your Labrador Retriever pup gives you the opportunity to show off your new friend, and your pup gets to reap the benefits of being an adorable furry creature that people will adore, want to pet and, in general, think is absolutely precious!

Besides getting to know his new family, your puppy should be exposed to other people, animals and situations. This will help him become well adjusted as he grows up and less prone to being timid or fearful of the new things he will encounter. Your pup's socialization began at the breeder's, and now it is your responsibility to continue it. The socialization he receives up until the age of 12 weeks is the most critical, as this is the time when he forms his impressions of the outside world. Lack of socialization can manifest itself in fear and aggression as the dog grows up. He needs lots of human contact, affection, handling and exposure to other animals. Be careful during the eight-to-ten-week-old period, also known as the fear period. The interaction he receives during this time should be gentle and reassuring.

Once your pup has received his necessary vaccinations, feel free to take him out and about (on his leash, of course). Take him

Lab puppies are very curious and "nosy"—they will investigate anything they can reach!

around the neighborhood, take him on your daily errands, let people pet him, let him meet other dogs and pets, etc. Puppies do not have to try to make friends; there will be no shortage of people who will want to introduce themselves. Just make sure that you carefully supervise each meeting. If the neighborhood children want to say hello, for example, that is great—children and pups most often make great companions. But sometimes an excited child can unintentionally handle a pup too roughly, or an overzealous pup can playfully nip a little too hard. You want to make socialization experiences positive ones; what a pup learns during this very formative stage will impact his

attitude toward future encounters. A pup that has a bad experience with a child may grow up to be a dog that is shy around or aggressive toward children, and you want your dog to be comfortable around everyone.

CONSISTENCY IN TRAINING
Dogs, being pack animals, naturally need a leader, or else they try to establish dominance in their packs. When you bring a dog into your family, who becomes the leader and who becomes the "pack" are entirely up to you! Your pup's intuitive quest for dominance, coupled with the fact that it is nearly impossible to look at an adorable Labrador Retriever pup, with his

"puppy-dog" eyes and sweet face, and not cave in, give the pup almost an unfair advantage in getting the upper hand! And a pup will definitely test the waters to see what he can and cannot get away with.

Do not give in to those pleading eyes—stand your ground when it comes to disciplining the pup and make sure that all family members do the same. It will only confuse the pup when Mother tells him to get off the couch when he is used to sitting up there with Father to watch the nightly news. Avoid discrepancies by having all members of the household decide on the rules before the pup even comes home…and be consistent in enforcing them! Early training shapes the dog's personality, so you cannot be unclear in what you expect.

COMMON PUPPY PROBLEMS

The best way to prevent problems is to be proactive in stopping an undesirable behavior as soon as it starts. The old saying "You can't teach an old dog new tricks" does not necessarily hold true, but it *is* true that it is much easier to discourage bad behavior in a young developing pup than to wait until the pup's bad behavior becomes the adult dog's bad habit. There are some problems that are especially prevalent in puppies as they develop.

NIPPING

As puppies start to teethe, they feel the need to sink their teeth into anything…unfortunately, that includes your fingers, arms, hair, toes…whatever happens to be available. You may find this behavior cute for about the first five seconds…until you feel just how sharp those puppy teeth are. This is something you want to discourage immediately and consistently with a firm "No!" (or whatever number of firm "Nos" it takes for him to understand that you mean business) and replace your finger with an appropriate chew toy. While this behavior is merely annoying when the dog is still young, it can become dangerous as your Labrador Retriever's adult teeth grow in and his jaws develop if he thinks that it is okay to gnaw on human appendages. Although the Labrador is bred to have a "soft" mouth, so as not to damage the game he retrieves, he can still cause a person great pain unintentionally with a friendly nip.

CRYING/WHINING

Your pup will often cry, whine, whimper, howl or make some type of commotion when he is left alone. This is basically his way of calling out for attention, of calling out to make sure that you know he is there and that you have not forgotten about him. He feels

It's hard to stand your ground when looking into the beguiling eyes of a Lab pup—and pups are quick to learn how to get their way!

THE PROBLEM CHILD

Training your puppy takes much patience and can be frustrating at times, but you should see results from your efforts. If you have a puppy that seems untrainable, take him to a trainer or behaviourist. The dog may have a personality problem that requires the help of a professional, or perhaps you need help in learning how to train your dog.

insecure when he is left alone; for example, when you are out of the house and he is in his crate or when you are in another part of the house and he cannot see you. The noise he is making is an expression of the anxiety he feels at being alone, so he needs to be taught that being alone is okay.

You are not actually training the dog to stop making noise, you are training him to feel comfortable when he is alone and thus removing the need for him to make the noise.

This is where the crate with a cozy blanket and a toy comes in handy. You want to know that your pup is safe when you are not there to supervise, and you know that he will be safe in his crate rather than roaming freely about the house. In order for the pup to stay in his crate without making a fuss, he needs to be comfortable in his crate. On that note, it is extremely important that the crate is never used as a form of punishment, or the pup will have a negative association with the crate.

Your Labrador Retriever puppy requires your guidance from the moment you bring him home.

With proper care and training, your cute, curious Lab puppy will grow into a beautiful, polite adult dog.

PUPPY FEEDING

You will probably start feeding your pup the same food that he has been getting from the breeder; the breeder should give you a few days' supply to start you off. Although you should not give your pup too many treats, you will want to have puppy treats on hand for coaxing, training, rewards, etc. Be careful, though, as a small pup's calorie requirements are relatively low and a few treats can add up to almost a full day's worth of calories without the required nutrition.

Accustom the pup to the crate in short, gradually increasing time intervals in which you put him in the crate, maybe with a treat, and stay in the room with him. If he cries or makes a fuss, do not go to him, but stay in his sight. Gradually he will realize that staying in his crate is all right without your help, and it will not be so traumatic for him when you are not around. You may want to leave the radio on softly when you leave the house; the sound of human voices may be comforting to him.

Shiny coat, alert demeanor and proper weight indicate that your dog is receiving proper nutrition and adequate exercise for good health.

FEEDING CONSIDERATIONS

You have probably heard it a thousand times: you are what you eat. Believe it or not, it's very true. For dogs, they are what you feed them because they have little choice in the matter. Even those people who truly want to feed their dogs the best often do not know which foods are best for their dogs and are overwhelmed by the many types of food available.

Dog foods are produced in three basic types: dry, semi-moist and canned. Dry foods are for the cost-conscious because they are much less expensive than semi-moist and canned. Dry foods contain the least fat and the most preservatives. Most canned foods are 60–70-percent water, while semi-moist foods are so full of sugar that they are the least preferred by owners, though dogs seem to welcome them.

Three stages of development must be considered when selecting a diet for your dog: the puppy stage, the adult stage and the senior stage.

PUPPY STAGE

Puppies have a natural instinct to nurse from their mother. They

FOOD SELECTION

Selecting the best dry dog food is difficult. There is no majority consensus among veterinary scientists as to the value of nutrient analysis (protein, fat, fiber, moisture, ash, cholesterol, minerals, etc.). All agree that feeding trials are what matter most, but you also have to consider the individual dog. The dog's weight, age and activity level, and what pleases his taste, all must be considered. It is probably best to take the advice of your veterinarian. Every dog's dietary requirements vary, even during the lifetime of a particular dog.

If your dog is fed a good dry food, it does not require supplements of meat or vegetables. Dogs do appreciate a little variety in their diets, so you may choose to stay with the same brand but vary the flavor. Alternatively, you may wish to add a little flavored stock to give a difference to the taste.

Establish a daily feeding schedule for your Lab, and feed him in a quiet corner where he can enjoy a peaceful meal.

should exhibit this behavior the first day of their lives. If they don't suckle within a few hours, the breeder should attempt to put them onto their mother's nipples. The pups' failure to feed means that the breeder will have to feed them himself under the advice and guidance of a veterinarian. Hand-feeding involves a baby bottle and a special formula. There are many good formulas available, but mother's milk is the best because it contains colostrum, a sort of antibiotic milk that protects the puppies during the first eight to ten weeks of their lives.

Puppies should be allowed to nurse for six weeks and they should be slowly weaned away from their mother by introducing small portions of canned meat after they are about one month old. By the time they are eight

Unless there is a problem, the puppy should nurse from its mother. Small bottles and milk formulas exist for feeding puppies that cannot suckle properly.

weeks old, they should be completely weaned and fed solely a puppy dry food. During the weaning period, selecting the best diet is most important, as the puppy grows fastest during the first year of life. Growth foods can be recommended by your veterinarian or breeder, and the puppy should be kept on this diet for up to about 18 months, depending on the individual dog's development.

Puppy and junior diets should be balanced for your dog's needs so that supplements of vitamins,

Multiple dogs mean multiple bowls! Each dog should have his own food and water bowls to ensure peaceful mealtimes and polite behavior.

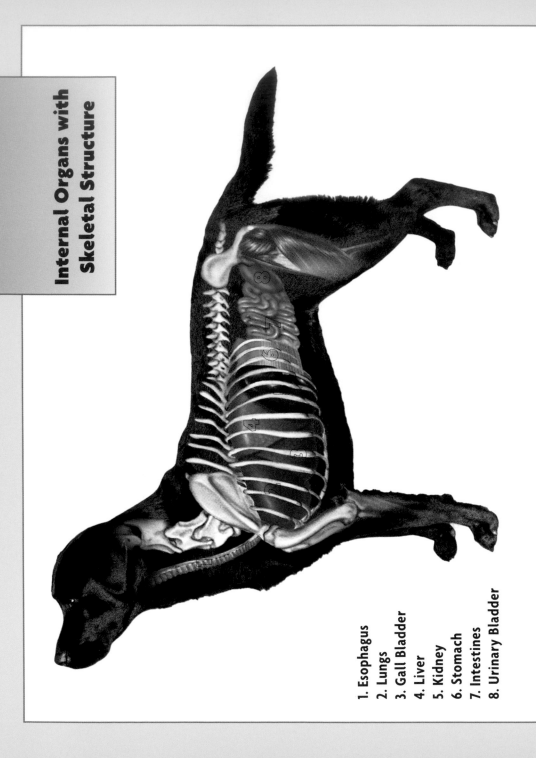

Internal Organs with Skeletal Structure

1. Esophagus
2. Lungs
3. Gall Bladder
4. Liver
5. Kidney
6. Stomach
7. Intestines
8. Urinary Bladder

minerals and protein should not be necessary.

ADULT DIETS
A dog is considered an adult when he has stopped growing. The growth is in height and/or length; do not consider the dog's weight when the decision is made to switch from a puppy diet to an adult-maintenance diet. Again you should rely upon your veterinarian to recommend an acceptable maintenance diet. Major dog food manufacturers specialize in this type of food and it is just necessary for you to select the one best suited to your dog's needs. Active dogs have different requirements than sedate dogs.

The time at which to switch a Lab to an adult diet varies from dog to dog. A Labrador Retriever generally reaches adulthood at about two years of age, though some dogs fully mature at 16 months, while others may take up to three years.

SENIOR DIETS
As dogs get older, their metabolism changes. The older dog usually exercises less, moves more slowly and sleeps more. This change in lifestyle and physiological performance requires a change in diet. Since these changes take place slowly, they might not be recognizable. What is easily recognizable is weight gain. By continuing to feed your dog an adult-maintenance

diet when he is slowing down metabolically, your dog will gain weight. Obesity in an older dog compounds the health problems that already accompany old age.

As your dog gets older, few of his organs function up to par. The kidneys slow down and the intestines become less efficient. These age-related factors are best handled with a change in diet and a change in feeding schedule to give smaller portions that are more easily digested.

There is no single best diet for every older dog. While many dogs do well on light or senior diets, other dogs do better on puppy diets or other special premium diets such as lamb and rice. Be sensitive to your senior Labrador Retriever's diet and this will help control other problems that may arise with your old friend.

Dogs are considered to be adults when they stop growing. Adult dogs should be fed a maintenance, rather than a puppy growth, food.

All Labs are active, but those that do vigorous exercise, such as field work or competition training, will have different dietary needs than their "homebody" counterparts.

WATER

Just as your dog needs proper nutrition from his food, water is an essential "nutrient" as well. Water keeps the dog's body properly hydrated and promotes normal function of the body's systems. During housebreaking, it is necessary to keep an eye on how much water your Labrador Retriever is drinking, but, once he is reliably trained, he should have access to clean fresh water at all times. Make sure that the dog's water bowl is clean, and change the water often.

EXERCISE

All dogs require some form of exercise, regardless of breed. A sedentary lifestyle is as harmful to a dog as it is to a person. The

Labrador Retriever happens to be an active breed that requires considerable exercise, but you don't have to be a weightlifter or marathon runner to provide your dog with the exercise he needs. Regular walks, play sessions in the yard or letting the dog run free in the fenced yard under your supervision are all sufficient forms of exercise for the Labrador Retriever. For those who are more ambitious, you will find that your Labrador Retriever will be able to keep up with you on extra-long walks, the morning run, or, of course, a swim.

Remember, not only is exercise essential to keep the dog's body fit, it is essential to his mental well-being. A bored dog will find something to do, which often manifests itself in some type of destructive behavior. In this sense, it is essential for the owner's mental well-being as well!

This Lab puppy looks surprised to have found an unexpected visitor at his water bowl.

GRAIN-BASED DIETS

Some less expensive dog foods are based on grains and other plant proteins. While these products may appear to be attractively priced, many breeders prefer diets based on animal proteins and believe that they are more conducive to your dog's health. Many grain-based diets rely on soy protein, which may cause flatulence (passing gas).

There are many cases, however, when your dog might require a special diet. These special requirements should only be recommended by your veterinarian.

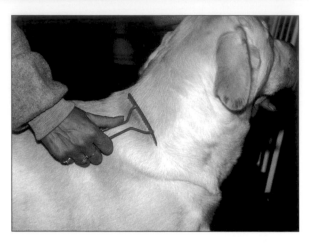

A wide-toothed metal rake is useful for removing dead hair, especially during shedding season.

GROOMING YOUR LAB

BRUSHING

A slicker brush, pin brush or metal comb can be used for regular routine grooming. Daily brushing is effective for removing dead hair and stimulating the dog's natural oils to add shine and a healthy look to the coat. Your Labrador Retriever is not a breed that needs excessive grooming, but his coat needs to be brushed daily as part of routine maintenance. Daily brushing will minimize mats, get rid of dust and dandruff and remove any dead hair. Regular grooming sessions are also a good way to spend time with your dog. Many dogs grow to like the feel of being brushed and will enjoy the daily routine.

BATHING

Dogs do not need to be bathed as often as humans, but occasional bathing is important for healthy skin and a shiny coat. Again, like most anything, if you accustom your pup to being bathed as a puppy, it will be second nature by the time he grows up. You want your dog to be at ease in the bath or else it could end up a wet, soapy, messy ordeal for both of you! Your Lab should take to water almost instantly, making bathing easier.

Brush your Labrador Retriever thoroughly before wetting his coat. This will get rid of most debris and dead hair, which are harder to remove when the coat is wet. Make sure that your dog has a good non-slip surface to stand on. Begin by wetting the dog's coat. A shower or hose attachment is necessary for thoroughly wetting and rinsing the coat. Check the water temperature to make sure that it is neither too hot nor too cold.

Next, apply shampoo to the dog's coat and work it into a good lather. You should purchase a shampoo that is made for dogs; do not use a product made for human hair. Wash the head last; you do not want shampoo to drip into the dog's eyes while you are washing the rest of his body. Work the shampoo all the way down to the skin. You can use this opportunity to check the skin for any bumps, bites or other abnormalities. Do not neglect any area of the body— get all of the hard-to-reach places.

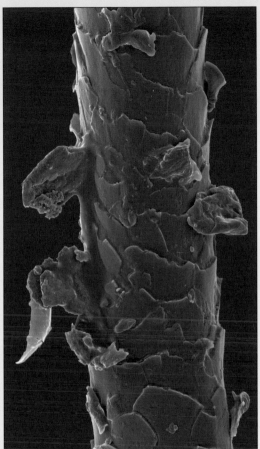

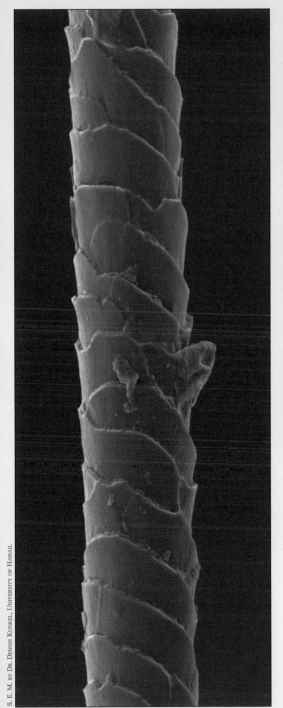

Scanning electron micrograph images of two hairs from a black Labrador Retriever. The hair to the left is a normal, healthy hair to which a few dead skin cells are clinging (part of dandruff). The cuticle (outer covering) is normal and uniform.

The hair shown above is an unhealthy hair, as evidenced by the damaged, uneven cuticle. These groundbreaking photos were taken by Dr. Dennis Kunkel at the University of Hawaii specifically for this book.

After a bath or a swim, you can rub your Lab with a heavy towel to soak up most of the water.

Once the dog has been thoroughly shampooed, he requires an equally thorough rinsing. Shampoo left in the coat can be irritating to the skin. Protect his eyes from the shampoo by shielding them with your hand and directing the flow of water in the opposite direction. You should also avoid getting water in the ear canal. Be prepared for your dog to shake out his coat—you might want to stand back, but make sure you have a hold on the dog to keep him from running through the house.

EAR CLEANING

The ears should be kept clean and any excess hair inside the ear should be trimmed. Ears can be cleaned with a cotton ball and special cleaner or ear powder made for dogs. Be on the lookout for any signs of infection or ear-mite infestation. If your Labrador Retriever has been shaking his head or scratching at his ears frequently, this usually indicates a problem. If his ears have an unusual odor, this is a sure sign of mite infestation or infection, and a signal to have his ears checked by the veterinarian.

NAIL CLIPPING

Your Labrador Retriever should be accustomed to having his nails trimmed at an early age, since it will be part of your maintenance routine throughout his life. Not only does it look nicer, but a dog with long nails can cause injury if

BATHING BEAUTY

Once you are sure that the dog is thoroughly rinsed, squeeze the excess water out of his coat with your hand and dry him with a heavy towel. You may choose to use a blow dryer on the "low" setting on his coat or just let it dry naturally. In cold weather, never allow your dog outside with a wet coat.

There are "dry bath" products on the market, which are sprays and powders intended for spot cleaning that can be used between regular baths if necessary. They are not substitutes for regular baths, but they are easy to use for touch-ups as they do not require rinsing.

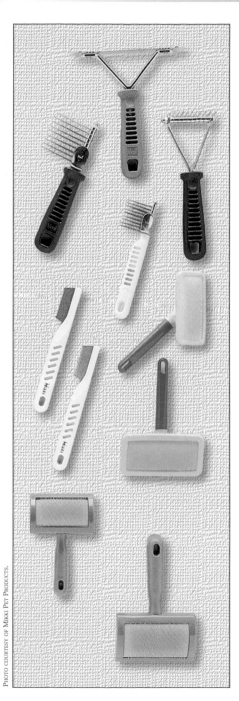

PHOTO COURTESY OF MIKKI PET PRODUCTS.

NAIL FILING

You can purchase an electric tool to grind down a dog's nails rather than cut them. Some dogs don't seem to mind the electric grinder but will object strongly to nail clippers. Talking it over with your veterinarian will help you make the right choice.

Your local pet shop will have a variety of useful grooming tools from which you can select what you need to maintain your Lab's coat.

he jumps up or if he scratches someone unintentionally. Also, a long nail has a better chance of ripping and bleeding, or causing the feet to spread. A good rule of thumb is that if you can hear your dog's nails' clicking on the floor when he walks, his nails are too long.

Before you start cutting, make sure you can identify the "quick" in each nail. The quick is a blood vessel that runs through the center of each nail and grows rather close to the end. It will bleed if accidentally cut, which will be quite painful for the dog as it contains

Cutting your Lab's nails requires gentle handling and care that the quick is not nipped in the process.

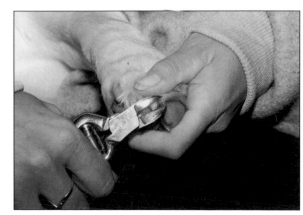

MOTION SICKNESS

*If life is a highway...*your dog may not want to come along for the ride! Some dogs experience motion sickness in cars that leads to excessive salivation and even vomiting. In most cases, your dog will fare better in the familiar, safe confines of his crate. To desensitize your dog, try going on several short jaunts before trying a long trip. If your dog experiences distress when riding in the vehicle, drive with him only when absolutely necessary, and do not feed him or give him water before you go.

Labrador Retrievers require minimal grooming, but they should be combed (with a metal comb) and/or brushed on a daily basis.

has calmed down, move on to the next nail. It is better to clip a little at a time, particularly with black-nailed dogs.

Hold your pup steady as you begin trimming his nails; you do not want him to make any sudden movements or run away. Talk to him soothingly and stroke his fur as you clip. Holding his foot in your hand, simply take off the end of each nail in one quick clip. You can purchase nail clippers that are specially made for dogs; you can probably find them wherever you buy grooming supplies.

ADDITIONAL GROOMING TIPS

Labrador Retrievers do not require elaborate haircuts or a lot of finishing work. Basically, the main goal in grooming the Labrador Retriever is to keep the dog's coat looking nice and in good health. During shedding season in the spring, you will need to pay a little more attention to his coat, but a vigorous brushing will suffice to loosen much of the dead hair in the undercoat. Follow up with a metal comb to remove the hair that is being cast off.

Some owners like to empha-size the otter-like look of the Labrador's tail by trimming it to give it a blunt point. Spray-on coat gloss is another optional grooming tool; this will give the Labrador's short, dense coat a

nerve endings. Keep some type of clotting agent on hand, such as a styptic pencil or styptic powder (the type used for shaving). This will stop the bleeding quickly when applied to the end of the cut nail. Do not panic if this happens, just stop the bleeding and talk soothingly to your dog. Once he

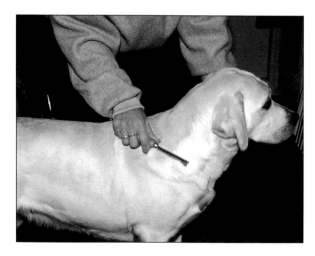

sleek sheen. An extra-shiny coat looks especially nice on black dogs.

TRAVELING WITH YOUR DOG

CAR TRAVEL

You should accustom your Labrador Retriever to riding in a car at an early age. You may or may not take him in the car often, but at the very least he will need to go to the vet and you do not want these trips to be traumatic for the dog or a big hassle for you. The safest way for a dog to ride in the car is in his crate. If he uses a fiberglass crate in the house, you can use the same crate for travel. If you have a wire crate in the house, consider purchasing an appropriately sized fiberglass or wooden crate for traveling. Wire crates can be used for travel, but fiberglass or wooden crates are sturdier and safer.

Put the pup in the crate and see how he reacts. If he seems

uneasy, you can have a passenger hold him on his lap while you drive. Another option is a specially made safety harness for dogs, which straps the dog in much like a seat belt. For larger vehicles, you can install a partition to section off the back of the vehicle and confine the dog. Do not let the dog roam loose in the vehicle—this is very dangerous! If you should stop short, your dog can be thrown and injured. If the dog starts climbing on you and pestering you while you are driving, you will not be able to concentrate on the road. It is an unsafe situation for everyone—human and canine.

For long trips, be prepared to stop to let the dog relieve himself. Bring along whatever you need to clean up after him, including some old towels and rags, should he have a potty accident in the car or suffer from

Never travel with your dog(s) freely roaming around your car. It is dangerous for both you and the dogs.

> ### TRAVEL ALERT!
> Never leave your dog alone in the car. In hot weather, your dog can die from the high temperature inside a closed vehicle; even a car parked in the shade can heat up very quickly. Leaving the window open is dangerous as well since the dog can hurt himself trying to get out.

GOING ABROAD

For international travel, you will have to make arrangements well in advance (perhaps months), as countries' regulations pertaining to bringing in animals differ. There may be special health certificates and/or vaccinations that your dog will need before taking the trip; sometimes this has to be done within a certain time frame. When traveling to rabies-free countries, you will need to bring proof of the dog's rabies vaccination and there will likely be a quarantine period upon arrival.

motion sickness. Also bring along some bottled water to offer to your Lab during the trip.

AIR TRAVEL

Contact your chosen airline before proceeding with your travel plans that include your Labrador Retriever. The dog will be required to travel in a fiberglass crate and you must always check in advance with the airline regarding specific requirements for the crate's size, type and labeling. To help put the dog at ease, give him one of his favorite toys in the crate. Do not feed the dog for several hours prior to checking in so that you minimize his need to relieve himself. However, some airlines require that the dog be fed within four hours of arriving at the airport, in which case a light meal is best. For long trips,

you will have to attach food and water bowls to the dog's crate so that airline employees can tend to him between legs of the trip.

Make sure that your dog is properly identified and that your contact information appears on his ID tags and on his crate. Your Lab will travel in a different area of the plane than the human passengers, so every rule must be strictly followed to prevent the risk of getting separated from your dog.

VACATIONS AND BOARDING

So you want to take a family vacation—and you want to include *all* members of the

COLLAR REQUIRED

If your dog gets lost, he is not able to ask for directions home. Identification tags fastened to the collar give important information—the dog's name, the owner's name, the owner's address and a telephone number where the owner can be reached. This makes it easy for whoever finds the dog to contact the owner and arrange to have the dog returned. An added advantage is that a person will be more likely to approach a lost dog who has ID tags on his collar; it tells the person that this is somebody's pet rather than a stray. This is the easiest and fastest method of identification, provided that the tags stay on the collar and the collar stays on the dog.

family. You would probably make arrangements for accommodations ahead of time anyway, but this is especially important when traveling with a dog. You do not want to make an overnight stop at the only place around for miles to find out that they do not allow dogs. Also, you do not want to reserve a place for your family without mentioning that you are bringing a dog because, if it is against their policy, you may not have a place to stay.

Alternatively, if you are traveling and choose not to bring your Labrador Retriever, you will have to make arrangements for him while you are away. Some options are to bring him to a neighbor's house to stay while you are gone, to have a trusted neighbor stop by often or stay at your house or to bring your dog to a reputable boarding kennel. If you choose to board him at a kennel, you should stop by to see the facility and where the dogs are kept to make sure that it is clean and spacious. Talk to some of the employees and see how they treat the dogs—do they spend time with the dogs, play with them, exercise them, etc.? You know that your Labrador Retriever will not be happy unless he gets regular activity. Also find out the kennel's policy on vaccinations and what they require. This is for all of the

There are many items available to help you care for your dog. An example is the special panties that are used for bitches in heat. It protects them from staining as well as having an unplanned mating.

dogs' safety, since when dogs are kept together, there is a greater risk of diseases being passed from dog to dog. Most facilities require the owner to provide current vaccination documentation.

IDENTIFICATION
Your Labrador Retriever is your valued companion and friend. That is why you always keep a close eye on him and you have made sure that he cannot escape from the garden or wriggle out of his collar and run away from you. However, accidents can happen and there may come a time when your dog unexpectedly gets separated from you. If this unfortunate event should occur, the first thing on your mind will be finding him. Proper identification, including ID tags and perhaps a microchip or tattoo, will increase the chances of his being returned to you safely and quickly.

TRAINING YOUR
LABRADOR RETRIEVER

Living with an untrained dog is a lot like owning a piano that you do not know how to play—it is a nice object to look at, but it does not do much more than that to bring you pleasure. Now try taking piano lessons, and suddenly the piano comes alive and brings forth magical sounds and rhythms that set your heart singing and your body swaying.

The same is true with your Labrador Retriever. At first you enjoy seeing him around the house. He does not do much with you other than to need food, water and exercise. Come to think of it, he does not bring you much joy, either. He is a big responsibility with a very small return. And often, he develops unacceptable behaviors that may annoy you, to say nothing of bad habits that may end up costing you great sums of money and a great deal of aggravation. Not a good thing!

Now train your Labrador Retriever. Enroll in an obedience class. Teach him good manners as you learn how and why he behaves the way he does. Find out how to communicate with your dog and how to recognize and understand his communications

with you. Suddenly the dog takes on a new role in your life—he is smart, interesting, well behaved and fun to be with, and he demonstrates his bond of devotion to you daily. In other words, your Labrador Retriever does wonders for your ego because he constantly reminds you that you are not only his leader, you are his hero! Miraculous things have happened—you have a wonderful dog (even your family and friends have noticed the transformation!) and you feel good about yourself.

Those involved with teaching dog obedience and counseling owners about their dogs' behavior have discovered some interesting facts about dog ownership. For example, training dogs when they are puppies results in the highest rate of success in developing well-mannered and well-adjusted adult dogs. Training an older dog, say from six months to six years of age, can produce almost equal results, providing that the owner accepts the dog's slower rate of learning capability and is willing to work patiently to help the dog succeed at developing to his fullest potential. Unfortunately, the patience factor is what many owners of untrained adult dogs lack, so they do not persist until their dogs are successful at learning particular behaviors.

Training a puppy, for example, aged 8 to 16 weeks (20 weeks at the most), is like working with a dry sponge in a pool of water. The pup soaks up whatever you show him and constantly looks for more things to do and learn. At this early age, his body is not yet producing hormones, and therein lies the reason for such a high rate of success. Without hormones, he is focused on his owners and not particularly interested in investigating other places, dogs, people, etc. You are his leader; his provider of food, water, shelter and security. Therefore, he latches onto you and wants to stay close. He will usually follow you from room to room, will not let you out of his sight when you are outdoors with him and will respond in like manner to the people and animals you encounter. If, for example, you greet a friend warmly, he will be happy to greet the person as well. If, however, you are hesitant or anxious about the approach of a stranger, he will respond accordingly.

Once the puppy begins to produce hormones, his natural curiosity emerges and he begins to investigate the world around him. It is at that time when you may

Much of the Lab's popularity stems from his trainability and inherent good nature.

notice that the untrained dog begins to wander away from you and even ignore your commands to stay close. When this behavior becomes a problem, you have two choices: get rid of the dog or train him. It is strongly urged that you choose the latter option.

Occasionally, there are no classes available within a reasonable distance from an owner's home. Sometimes there are classes available but the tuition is too costly. Whatever the circumstances, the solution to training the Lab without formal lessons lies within the pages of this book.

This chapter is devoted to helping you train your Labrador Retriever at home. If the recommended procedures are followed

THINK BEFORE YOU BARK

Dogs are sensitive to their masters' moods and emotions. Use your voice wisely when communicating with your dog. Never raise your voice at your dog unless you are trying to correct him. "Barking" at your dog can become as meaningless as "dogspeak" is to you.

faithfully, you may expect positive results that will prove rewarding to both you and your dog.

Whether your Labrador Retriever is a puppy or a mature adult, the methods of teaching and the techniques we use in training basic behaviors are the same. After all, no dog, whether puppy or adult, likes harsh or inhumane methods. All creatures, however, respond favorably to gentle motivational methods and sincere praise and encouragement. Now let us get started.

HOUSEBREAKING

You can train a puppy to relieve himself wherever you choose. For example, city dwellers often train their puppies to relieve themselves on the sidewalk because large plots of grass are not readily available. Of course, these people must bring a "poop-scoop" along on walks to clean up any droppings immediately. Suburbanites, on the other hand, usually have yards to accommodate their dogs' needs.

Outdoor training includes such surfaces as grass, dirt and cement. Indoor training usually means training your dog to newspaper, not a very feasible option with a large dog like the Lab.

When deciding on the surface and location that you will want your Labrador Retriever to use, be sure it is going to be permanent. Training your dog to grass and then changing your mind two months later is extremely difficult for both dog and owner.

Next, choose the command you will use each and every time you want your puppy to void. "Hurry up" and "Let's go" are examples of commands commonly used by dog owners.

Get in the habit of asking the puppy, "Do you want to go hurry up?" (or whatever your chosen relief command is) before you take him out. That way, when he becomes an adult, you will be able to determine if he wants to go out when you ask him. A confirmation will be signs of interest such as wagging his tail, watching you intently, going to the door, etc.

PUPPY'S NEEDS

The puppy needs to relieve himself after play periods, after each meal, after he has been sleeping and any time he indicates that he is looking for a place to urinate or defecate.

The urinary and intestinal tract muscles of very young puppies are not fully developed. Therefore, like human babies, puppies need to relieve themselves frequently. Take your puppy out often—every hour for an eight-week-old, for example. The older the puppy, the less often he will need to relieve himself. Finally, as a mature healthy adult, he will require only three to five relief trips per day.

HOUSING

Since the types of housing and control you provide for your puppy have a direct relationship on the success of house-training, we consider the various aspects of both before we begin training.

Bringing a new puppy home and turning him loose in your house can be compared to turning a child loose in a sports arena and telling the child that the place is all his! The sheer enormity of the place would be too much for him to handle.

Instead, offer the puppy clearly defined areas where he can play, sleep, eat and live. A room of the house where the family gathers is the most obvious choice. Puppies are social animals and need to feel a part of the pack right from the start. Hearing your voice, watching you while you are doing things and smelling you nearby are all positive reinforcers that he is now a member of your

It won't take long before your Lab knows the routine and he'll let you know when it's time "to go."

pack. Usually a family room, the kitchen or a nearby adjoining breakfast nook is ideal for providing safety and security for both puppy and owner.

Within that room, there should be a smaller area that the puppy can call his own. A wire or fiberglass dog crate or a partitioned-off (not boarded!) corner from which he can view the activities of his new family will be fine. The size of the area or crate is the key factor here. The area must be large enough for the puppy to lay down and stretch out as well as stand up without rubbing his head on the top, yet small enough so that he cannot relieve himself at one end and sleep at the other without coming into contact with his droppings during the housebreaking process.

Dogs are, by nature, clean animals and will not remain close to their relief areas unless forced to do so. In those cases, they then become dirty dogs and usually remain that way for life.

The crate or area should be lined with a clean towel or soft mat and offer one toy, no more. Do not put food or water in the crate during house-training, as eating and drinking will activate his digestive processes and ulti-mately defeat your purpose as well as make the puppy very uncomfortable as he attempts to "hold it."

THE CLEAN LIFE

By providing sleeping and resting quarters that fit the dog, and offering frequent opportunities to relieve himself outside his quarters, the puppy quickly learns that the outdoors is the place to go when he needs to urinate or defecate. It also reinforces his innate desire to keep his sleeping quarters clean. This, in turn, helps develop the muscle control that will eventually produce a dog with clean living habits.

CONTROL

By control, we mean helping the puppy to create a lifestyle pattern that will be compatible to that of his human pack (*you*!). Just as we guide little children to learn our way of life, we must show the puppy when it is time to play, eat, sleep, exercise and even entertain himself.

Your puppy should always sleep in his crate. He should also learn that, during times of household confusion and excessive human activity such as at breakfast when family members are preparing for the day, he can play by himself in relative safety and comfort in his crate. Each time you leave the puppy alone, he should be crated. Puppies are chewers. They cannot tell the difference between safe chew toys and lamp cords, television wires, shoes, table legs, etc. Chewing into a television wire, for example, can be fatal to the puppy, while a shorted wire can start a fire in the house.

If the puppy chews on the chair when he is alone, you will probably discipline him angrily when you get home. Thus, he makes the association that your coming home means he is going to be hit or punished. (He will not remember chewing up the chair and is incapable of making the association of the discipline with his naughty deed.) Crating the pup prevents this from happening.

Times of excitement, such as family parties, neighbors' visits etc., can be fun for the puppy, providing he can view the activities from the security of his crate. He is not underfoot and he is not being fed all sorts of tidbits that will probably cause him stomach distress, yet he still feels a part of the fun.

SCHEDULE

As stated earlier, a puppy should be taken to his relief area each time he is released from his crate, after meals, after play sessions, when he first awakens in the morning (at age 8 weeks, this can mean 5 a.m.!) and whenever he indicates by circling or sniffing busily that he needs to urinate or defecate. For a puppy less than ten weeks of age, a routine of taking him out every hour is necessary. As the puppy grows, he will be able to wait for longer periods of time.

Keep trips to his relief area short. Stay no more than five or six minutes and then return to the house. If he goes during that time, praise him lavishly and take him indoors immediately. If he does not, but he has an accident when you go back indoors, pick him up immediately, say "No! No!" and return to his relief area. Wait a few minutes, then return to the house again. *Never* hit a puppy or put his face in urine or excrement when he has an accident!

Once indoors, put the puppy in his crate until you have had time to clean up his accident. Then release him to the family area and watch him more closely than before. Chances are, his accident was a result of your not picking up his signal or waiting

THE SUCCESS METHOD

Success that comes by luck is usually short-lived. Success that comes by well-thought-out proven methods is often more easily achieved and permanent. The method of crate training presented here is the Success Method. It is designed to give you, the puppy owner, a simple yet proven way to help your puppy develop clean living habits and a feeling of security in his new environment.

Canine Development Schedule

It is important to understand how and at what age a puppy develops into adulthood. If you are a puppy owner, consult the following Canine Development Schedule to determine the stage of development your Labrador Retriever puppy is currently experiencing. This knowledge will help you as you work with the puppy in the weeks and months ahead.

Period	Age	Characteristics
FIRST TO THIRD	BIRTH TO SEVEN WEEKS	Puppy needs food, sleep and warmth, and responds to simple and gentle touching. Needs mother for security and disciplining. Needs littermates for learning and interacting with other dogs. Pup learns to function within a pack and learns pack order of dominance. Begin socializing pup with adults and children for short periods. Pup begins to become aware of his environment.
FOURTH	EIGHT TO TWELVE WEEKS	Brain is fully developed. Needs socializing with outside world. Remove from mother and littermates. Needs to change from canine pack to human pack. Human dominance necessary. Fear period occurs between 8 and 16 weeks. Avoid fright and pain.
FIFTH	THIRTEEN TO SIXTEEN WEEKS	Training and formal obedience should begin. Less association with other dogs, more with people, places, situations. Period will pass easily if you remember this is pup's change-to-adolescence time. Be firm and fair. Flight instinct prominent. Permissiveness and over-disciplining can do permanent damage. Praise for good behavior.
JUVENILE	FOUR TO EIGHT MONTHS	Another fear period about 7 to 8 months of age. It passes quickly, but be cautious of fright and pain. Sexual maturity reached. Dominant traits established. Dog should understand sit, down, come and stay by now.

NOTE: THESE ARE APPROXIMATE TIME FRAMES. ALLOW FOR INDIVIDUAL DIFFERENCES IN PUPPIES.

too long before offering him the opportunity to relieve himself. *Never* hold a grudge against the puppy for accidents.

Let the puppy learn that going outdoors means it is time to relieve himself, not play. Once trained, he will be able to play indoors and out and still differentiate between the times for play versus the times for relief.

Help the puppy develop regular hours for naps, being alone, playing by himself and just resting, all in his crate. Encourage him to entertain himself while you are busy with your activities. Let

him learn that having you near is comforting, but it is not your main purpose in life to provide him with your undivided attention.

Each time you put the puppy in his crate, tell him "Crate time!" (or whatever command you choose). Soon, he will run to his crate when he hears you say those words.

In the beginning of his training, do not leave him in his crate for prolonged periods of time except during the night when everyone is sleeping. Make his experience with his crate a pleasant one and, as an adult, he

THE SUCCESS METHOD
6 Steps to Successful Crate Training

1 Tell the puppy "Crate time!" and place him in the crate with a small treat (a piece of cheese or half of a biscuit). Let him stay in the crate for five minutes while you are in the same room. Then release him and praise lavishly. Never release him when he is fussing. Wait until he is quiet before you let him out.

2 Repeat Step 1 several times a day.

3 The next day, place the puppy in the crate as before. Let him stay there for ten minutes. Do this several times.

4 Continue building time in five-minute increments until the puppy

stays in his crate for 30 minutes with you in the room. Always take him to his relief area after prolonged periods in his crate.

5 Now go back to Step 1 and let the puppy stay in his crate for five minutes, this time while you are out of the room.

6 Once again, build crate time in five-minute increments with you out of the room. When the puppy will stay willingly in his crate (he may even fall asleep!) for 30 minutes with you out of the room, he will be ready to stay in it for several hours at a time.

PAPER CAPER

Never line your pup's sleeping area with newspaper. Puppy litters are usually raised on newspaper and, once in your home, the puppy will immediately associate newspaper with voiding. Never put newspaper on any floor while house-training, as this will only confuse the puppy. Finally, restrict water intake after evening meals. Offer a few licks at a time—never let a young puppy gulp water after meals. In fact, Labs of any age should not gulp water; gulping increases the risk of bloat.

will love his crate and willingly stay in it for several hours. There are millions of people who go to work every day and leave their adult dogs crated while they are away. The dogs accept this as their lifestyle and look forward to "crate time."

Crate training provides safety for you, the puppy and the home. It also provides the puppy with a feeling of security, and that helps the puppy achieve self-confidence and clean habits.

Remember that one of the primary ingredients in house-training your puppy is control. Regardless of your lifestyle, there will always be occasions when you will need to have a place where your dog can stay and be happy and safe. Crate training is the answer for now and in the future.

In conclusion, a few key elements are really all you need for a successful house- and crate-training method—consistency, frequency, praise, control and supervision. By following these procedures with a normal, healthy puppy, you and the puppy will soon be past the stage of "accidents" and ready to move on to a full and rewarding life together.

ROLES OF DISCIPLINE, REWARD AND PUNISHMENT

Discipline, training one to act in accordance with rules, brings order to life. It is as simple as that. Without discipline, particularly in a group society, chaos reigns supreme and the group will eventually perish. Humans and canines are social animals and need some form of discipline in order to function effectively. They must procure food, reproduce to keep the species going and protect their home base and their young.

If there were no discipline in the lives of social animals, they would eventually die from starvation and/or predation by stronger animals. In the case of domestic canines, dogs need discipline in their lives in order to understand how their pack (you and other family members) functions and how they must act in order to survive.

A large humane society in a highly populated area recently surveyed dog owners regarding their satisfaction with their relationships with their dogs. People who had trained their dogs were 75% more satisfied with their pets than those who had never trained their dogs.

Dr. Edward Thorndike, a noted psychologist, established *Thorndike's Theory of Learning*, which states that a behavior that results in a pleasant event tends to be repeated. A behavior that results in an unpleasant event tends not to be repeated. It is this theory on which training methods are based today. For example, if you manipulate a dog to perform a specific behavior and reward him for doing it, he is likely to do it again because he enjoyed the end result.

Occasionally, punishment, a penalty inflicted for an offense, is necessary. The best type of punishment often comes from an outside source. For example, a child is told not to touch the stove because he may get burned. He disobeys and touches the stove. In doing so, he receives a burn. From that time on, he respects the heat of the stove and avoids contact with it. Therefore, a behavior that results in an unpleasant event tends not to be repeated.

A good example of a dog learning the hard way is the dog who chases the house cat. He is told many times to leave the cat

CONSISTENCY PAYS OFF

Dogs need consistency in their feeding schedule, exercise and relief visits, and in the verbal commands you use. If you use "Stay" on Monday and "Stay here, please" on Tuesday, you will confuse your dog. Don't demand perfect behavior during training sessions and then let him have the run of the house the rest of the day. Above all, lavish praise on your pet consistently every time he does something right. The more he feels he is pleasing you, the more willing he will be to learn.

alone, yet he persists in teasing the cat. Then, one day he begins chasing the cat but the cat turns and swipes a claw across the dog's face, leaving him with a painful gash on his nose. The final result is that the dog stops chasing the cat.

TRAINING EQUIPMENT

COLLAR
A simple buckle collar is fine for most dogs. One who pulls mightily on the leash may require a chain choker collar. Only in the most severe cases of a dog's being totally out of control is it recommended to use a prong or pinch collar, and in this case only if the owner has been instructed in the proper use of such equipment. You likely will not need to resort to this with your Labrador.

LEASH
A 6-foot leash is recommended, preferably made of leather or

nylon. A chain leash is not recommended, as many dog owners find that the chain cuts into their hands and that switching the leash back and forth frequently between their hands is painful.

TREATS
Have a bag of treats on hand. Something nutritious and easy to swallow works best; use a soft treat, a chunk of cheese or a piece of cooked chicken rather than a dry biscuit. By the time the dog gets done chewing a dry treat, he will forget why he is being rewarded in the first place! Using food rewards will not teach a dog to beg at the table—the only way to teach a dog to beg at the table is to give him food from the table. In training, rewarding the dog with a food treat away from the

table will help him associate praise and the treats with learning new behaviors that obviously please his owner.

TRAINING BEGINS: ASK THE DOG A QUESTION

In order to teach your dog anything, you must first get his attention. After all, he cannot learn anything if he is looking away from you with his mind on something else.

To get his attention, ask him "School?" and immediately walk over to him and give him a treat as you tell him "Good dog." Wait a minute or two and repeat the routine, this time with a treat in your hand as you approach the dog to within a foot of him. Do not go directly to him, but stop about a foot short of him and hold out the treat as you ask "School?" He will see you approaching with a treat in your hand and most likely begin walking toward you. As you meet, give him the treat and praise again.

The third time, ask the question, have a treat in your hand and walk only a short distance toward the dog so that he must walk almost all the way to you. As he reaches you, give him the treat and praise again.

By this time, the dog will probably be getting the idea that if he pays attention to you, especially when you ask that question, it will pay off in treats

and fun activities for him. In other words, he learns that "school" means doing fun things with you that result in treats and positive attention for him.

Remember that the dog does not understand your verbal language, he only recognizes sounds. Your question translates to a series of sounds for him, and those sounds become the signal to go to you and pay attention; if he does, he will get to interact with you plus receive treats and praise.

Labs are easily motivated with food in training, but eventually they must be weaned from continual food rewards.

Good sit!," etc. Remember to always praise enthusiastically, because dogs relish verbal praise from their owners and feel so proud of themselves whenever they accomplish a behavior.

You will not use food forever in getting the dog to obey your commands. Food is only used to teach new behaviors, and once the dog knows what you want when you give a specific command, you will wean him off of the food treats but still maintain the verbal praise. After all, you will always have your voice with you, but there will be many times when you have no food rewards yet you expect the dog to obey.

A little pressure on the dog's rear will help him assume the correct sit position for the first few times, and from there he should learn the command quickly.

THE BASIC COMMANDS

TEACHING SIT

Now that you have the dog's attention, hold the leash in your left hand and the food treat in your right. Place your food hand at the dog's nose and let him lick the treat but not take it from you. Say "Sit" and slowly raise your food hand from in front of the dog's nose to up over his head so that he is looking at the ceiling. As he bends his head upward, he will have to bend his knees to maintain his balance. As he bends his knees, he will assume a sit position. At that point, release the food treat and praise lavishly with comments such as "Good dog!

Teaching the down can be accomplished easily with encouragement and motivation— and a treat surely helps!

TEACHING DOWN

Teaching the down exercise is easy when you understand how the dog perceives the down position, and it is very difficult when you do not. In addition, teaching the down exercise using the wrong method can sometimes make the dog develop such a fear of the down that he either runs away when you say "Down" or he attempts to bite the person who tries to force him down.

Have the dog sit close alongside your left leg, facing in the same direction as you are. Hold the leash in your left hand and a food treat in your right. Now place your left hand lightly on the top of the dog's shoulders where they meet above the spinal cord. Do not push down on the dog's shoulders; simply rest your left hand there so you can guide the dog to lie down close to your left leg rather than to swing away from your side when he drops.

Now place the food hand at the dog's nose, say "Down" very softly (almost a whisper) and slowly lower the food hand to the dog's front feet. When the food hand reaches the floor, begin moving it forward along the floor in front of the dog. Keep talking softly to the dog, saying things like, "Do you want this treat? You can do this, good dog." Your reassuring tone of voice will help calm the dog as he tries to follow

during the teaching process as we help the dog to understand exactly what it is that we are expecting him to do.

To teach the sit/stay, start with the dog sitting on your left side as before and hold the leash in your left hand. Have a food treat in your right hand and place your food hand at the dog's nose. Say "stay" and step out on your right foot to stand directly in front of the dog, toe to toe, as he licks and nibbles the treat. Be sure to keep his head facing upward to maintain the sit position. Count to five and then swing around to stand next to the dog again with him on your left. As soon as you get back to the original position, release the food and praise lavishly.

To teach the down/stay, do the down as previously described. As soon as the dog lies down, say "stay" and step out on your right foot just as you did in the sit/stay. Count to five and then return to stand beside the dog with him on

The stay command is taught in increments. Gradually add time and distance between you and your dog as you practice the stay command.

the food hand in order to get the treat.

When the dog's elbows touch the floor, release the food and praise softly. Try to get the dog to maintain that down position for several seconds before you let him sit up again. The goal here is to get the dog to settle down and not feel threatened in the down position.

TEACHING STAY
It is easy to teach the dog to stay in either a sit or a down position. Again, we use food and praise

---

DOUBLE JEOPARDY

A dog in jeopardy never lies down. He stays alert on his feet because instinct tells him that he may have to run away or fight for his survival. Therefore, if a dog feels threatened or anxious, he will not lie down. Consequently, it is important to keep the dog calm and relaxed as he learns the down exercise.

your left side. Release the treat and praise as always.

Within a week or ten days, you can begin to add a bit of distance between you and your dog when you leave him. When you do, use your left hand open with the palm facing the dog as a stay signal, much the same as the hand signal a police officer uses to stop traffic at an intersection. Hold the food treat in your right hand as before, but this time the food is not touching the dog's nose. He will watch the food hand and quickly learn that he is going to get that treat as soon as you return to his side.

When you can stand 1 yard away from your dog for 30 seconds, you can then begin building time and distance in both stays. Eventually, the dog can be expected to remain in the stay position for prolonged periods of time until you return to him or call him to you. Always praise lavishly when he stays.

TEACHING COME

If you make teaching "come" a fun experience, you should never have a "student" that does not love the game or that fails to come when called. The secret, it seems, is never to teach the word "come."

At times when an owner most wants his dog to come when called, the owner is likely upset or anxious and he allows these

feelings to come through in the tone of his voice when he calls his dog. Hearing that desperation in his owner's voice, the dog fears the results of going to him and therefore either disobeys outright or runs in the opposite direction. The secret, therefore, is to teach the dog a game and, when you want him to come to you, simply play the game. It is practically a no-fail solution!

To begin, have several members of your family take a few food treats and each go into a different room in the house. Take turns calling the dog, and each person should celebrate the dog's finding him with a treat and lots of happy praise. When a person calls the dog, he is actually inviting the dog to find him and get a treat as a reward for "winning" the game.

Teaching your Lab to retrieve is building on a natural tendency. Labs *love* to retrieve, and you can combine fetching games with teaching the dog to come.

A few turns of the "Where are you?" game and the dog will figure out that everyone is playing the game and that each person has a big celebration awaiting the dog's success at locating him. Once the dog learns to love the game, simply calling out "Where are you?" will bring him running from wherever he is when he hears that all-important question.

The come command is recognized as one of the most important things to teach a dog, so it is interesting to note that there are trainers who work with thousands of dogs and never teach the actual word "come." Yet these dogs will race to respond to a person who uses the dog's name followed by "Where are you?" In one instance, for example, a woman has a 12-year-old companion dog who went blind, but who never fails to locate her owner when asked, "Where are you?"

Children particularly love to play this game with their dogs. Children can hide in smaller places like a shower or bathtub, behind a bed or under a table. The dog needs to work a little bit harder to find these hiding places, but when he does he loves to celebrate with a treat and a tussle with a favorite youngster.

TEACHING HEEL

Heeling means that the dog walks beside the owner without pulling. It takes time and patience on the owner's part to succeed at teaching the dog that he (the owner) will not proceed unless the dog is walking calmly beside him. Pulling out ahead on the leash is definitely not acceptable.

Begin with holding the leash in your left hand as the dog sits beside your left leg. Hold the loop end of the leash in your right hand but keep your left hand short on the leash so it keeps the dog in close next to you.

Say "heel" and step forward on your left foot. Keep the dog close to you and take three steps. Stop and have the dog sit next to you in what we now call the heel position. Praise verbally, but do not touch the dog. Hesitate a moment and begin again with "heel," taking three steps and stopping, at which point the dog is told to sit again.

PLAN TO PLAY

The puppy should have regular play and exercise sessions when he is with you or a family member. Exercise for a very young puppy can consist of a short walk around the house or yard. Playing can include fetching games with a large ball or a special toy. (All puppies teethe and need soft things upon which to chew.) Remember to restrict play periods to indoors within his living area (the family room, for example) until he is completely house-trained.

Your goal here is to have the dog walk those three steps without pulling on the leash. When he will walk calmly beside you for three steps without pulling, increase the number of steps you take to five. When he will walk politely beside you while you take five steps, you can increase the length of your walk to ten steps. Keep increasing the length of your stroll until the dog will walk quietly beside you without pulling as long as you want him to heel. When you stop heeling, indicate to the dog that the exercise is over by verbally praising as you pet him and say "OK, good dog." The "OK" is used as a release word, meaning that the exercise is finished and the dog is free to relax.

If you are dealing with a dog who insists on pulling you around, simply "put on your brakes" and stand your ground until the dog realizes that the two of you are not going anywhere until he is beside you and moving at your pace, not his. It may take some time just standing there to convince the dog that you are the leader and you will be the one to decide on the direction and speed of your travel.

Each time the dog looks up at you or slows down to give a slack lead between the two of you, quietly praise him and say, "Good heel. Good dog."

HEELING WELL
Teach your dog to heel in an enclosed area. Once you think the dog will obey reliably and you want to attempt advanced obedience exercises such as off-lead heeling, test him in a fenced-in area so he cannot run away.

Eventually, the dog will begin to respond and within a few days he will be walking politely beside you without pulling on the leash. At first, the training sessions should be kept short and very positive; soon the dog will be able to walk nicely with you for increasingly longer distances. Remember also to give the dog free time and the opportunity to run and play when you are done with heel practice.

Perhaps the most natural activity for a Lab to learn is retrieving in water. Usually he won't be able to wait to jump in!

WEANING OFF FOOD TREATS

Food is used in training new behaviors, yet once the dog understands what behavior goes with a specific command, it is time to start weaning him off the food treats. At first, give a treat after each exercise. Then, start to give a treat only after every other exercise. Mix up the times when you offer a food reward and the times when you only offer praise so that the dog will never know when he is going to receive both food and praise and when he is going to receive only praise. This is called a variable ratio reward system and it proves successful because there is always the chance that the owner will produce a treat, so the dog never stops trying for that reward. No matter what, *always* give verbal praise.

OBEDIENCE CLASSES

As previously discussed, it is a good idea to enroll in an obedience class if one is available in your area. Many areas have dog clubs that offer basic obedience

NATURAL PRODIGY

Occasionally, a dog and owner who have not attended formal classes have been able to earn entry-level titles by obtaining competition rules and regulations from a local kennel club and practising on their own to a degree of perfection. Obtaining the higher level titles, however, almost always requires extensive training under the tutelage of experienced instructors. In addition, the more difficult levels require more specialized equipment whereas the lower levels do not.

training as well as preparatory classes for obedience competition. There are also local dog trainers who offer similar classes. If yours is a show dog, you may consider preparatory classes for showing.

At obedience trials, Labs are very successful and can earn titles at various levels of competition. The beginning levels of competition include basic behaviors such as sit, down, heel, etc. The more advanced levels of competition include jumping, retrieving, scent discrimination and signal work. The advanced levels require a dog and owner to put a lot of time and effort into their training; the titles that can be earned at these levels of competition are very prestigious.

OTHER ACTIVITIES FOR LIFE

Whether a dog is trained in the structured environment of a class or alone with his owner at home, there are many activities that can bring fun and rewards to both owner and dog once they have mastered basic control. The Labrador Retriever is one of the most tractable breeds around, and thus has earned the distinction of frequently being trained for guide-dog and service work. This tractability also translates into a pet dog who can be trained to do many things with his owner.

Teaching the dog to help out around the home, in the yard or on the farm provides great satisfaction to both dog and owner. In addition, the dog's help makes life a little easier for his owner and raises his stature as a valued companion to his family. It helps give the dog a purpose; it helps to keep his mind occupied and provides an outlet for his energy.

Backpacking is an exciting and healthful activity that the dog can be taught without assistance from more than his owner. The exercise of walking and climbing is good for man and dog alike, and the bond that they develop together is priceless. The rule of thumb is not to allow the dog to carry more than one-sixth of his body weight.

Labrador Retrievers have been very successfully used as guide dogs for the blind.

Yellow Labrador being trained for guide-dog work at The Seeing Eye®, Morristown, NJ.

If you are interested in participating in organized competition with your Labrador Retriever, there are other activities other than obedience in which you and your dog can become involved. Agility is a popular and fun sport in which dogs run through an obstacle course that includes various jumps, tunnels and other exercises to test the dog's speed and coordination. The owners run through the course beside their dogs to give commands and to guide the dogs through the course. Although competitive, the focus is on fun—it's fun to do and fun to watch, as well as great exercise.

Field trials, hunting trials and water tests are also popular with

owners of retriever breeds, since these activities are designed to test the dogs' innate instincts. These trials evaluate the Labrador's ability as a hunter and retriever, the breed's original roles.

Up and over the dog walk at an agility trial. The athletic, trainable Lab is a natural at the sport of agility.

HEALTH CARE OF YOUR
LABRADOR RETRIEVER

Dogs suffer from many of the same physical illnesses as people. They might even share many of the same psychological problems. Since people usually know more about human diseases than canine maladies, many of the terms used in this chapter will be familiar but not necessarily those used by veterinarians. We will use the term *x-ray*, instead of the more acceptable term *radiograph*. We will also use the familiar term *symptoms* even though dogs don't have symptoms, which are verbal descriptions of the patient's feelings; dogs have *clinical signs*. Since dogs can't speak, we have to look for clinical signs...but we still use the term *symptoms* in this book.

As a general rule, medicine is *practiced*. That term is not arbitrary. Medicine is a constantly changing art as we learn more and more about genetics, electronic aids (like CAT scans and MRIs) and daily laboratory advances. There are many dog maladies, like canine hip dysplasia, which are not universally treated in the same manner. For example, some veterinarians opt for surgical treatment more often than others do.

Your veterinarian will be your Lab's friend throughout the dog's life.

SELECTING A QUALIFIED VETERINARIAN

Your selection of a veterinarian should be based not only upon his personality and skills but also upon his convenience to your home. You require a veterinarian who is close by because you might have emergencies or need to make multiple visits for treatments. You should select a vet who has services that you might require such as tattooing and boarding, as well as a good reputation for ability and responsiveness. There is nothing more frustrating than having to wait a day or more to get a response from your veterinarian when time is of the essence. You should seek a vet who has experience with the Labrador Retriever, which should not be too difficult.

All veterinarians are licensed and their diplomas and/or certificates should be displayed in their waiting rooms. There are, however, many veterinary specialties that usually require further studies and internships. There are specialists in heart problems (veterinary cardiologists), skin problems (veterinary dermatologists), teeth and gum problems (veterinary dentists), eye problems (veterinary ophthalmologists) and x-rays (veterinary radiologists), as well as surgeons who have specialties in bones, muscles or certain organs. Most veterinarians do routine surgery such as neutering, stitching up wounds and docking tails for those breeds in which such is required for show purposes.

When the problem affecting your dog is serious, it is not unusual or impudent to get another medical opinion, although it is courteous to advise the vets concerned about this. You might also want to compare costs among several veterinarians. Sophisticated health care and veterinary services can be very costly. Don't be bashful about discussing these costs with your veterinarian or his staff. Financial considerations often play a role in deciding on a course of treatment.

PREVENTATIVE MEDICINE
It is much easier, less costly and more effective to practice preventative medicine than to fight bouts of illness and disease.

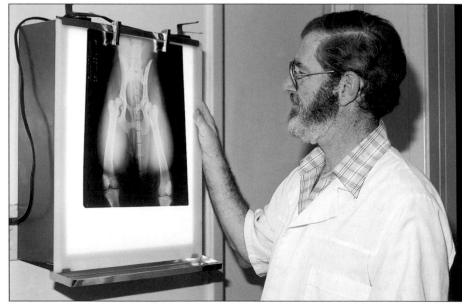

You should select a vet who is familiar with the Lab and the potential problems specific to the breed. X-ray examinations for hip dysplasia, for example, will be an important part of your Lab's care.

Normal Canine Skeleton

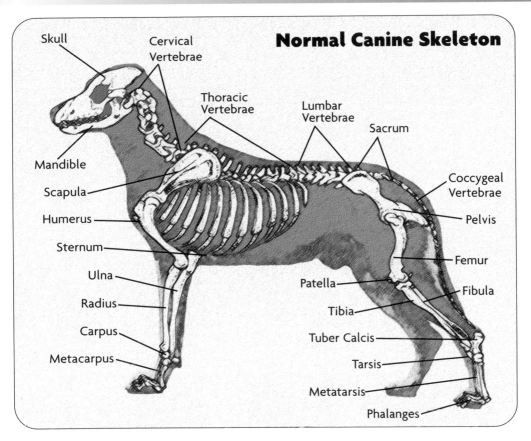

Skull
Cervical Vertebrae
Thoracic Vertebrae
Lumbar Vertebrae
Sacrum
Mandible
Scapula
Humerus
Sternum
Ulna
Radius
Carpus
Metacarpus
Coccygeal Vertebrae
Pelvis
Femur
Patella
Fibula
Tibia
Tuber Calcis
Tarsis
Metatarsis
Phalanges

Properly bred puppies come from parents that were selected based upon their genetic disease profiles. Their mother should have been vaccinated, free of all internal and external parasites and properly nourished. For these reasons, a visit to the veterinarian who cared for the dam (mother) is recommended. The dam can pass on disease resistance to her puppies. This resistance can last for eight to ten weeks. She can also pass on parasites and many infections. That's why it is helpful to know as much about the dam's health as possible.

WEANING TO FIVE MONTHS OLD
Puppies should be weaned by the time they are about two months old. A puppy that remains for at least eight weeks with his mother and littermates usually adapts better to other dogs and people later in his life.

In every case, you should have your newly acquired puppy examined by a veterinarian immediately. Vaccination programs usually begin when the puppy is very young.

The puppy will have his teeth examined, have his skeletal conformation checked and have his general health checked prior to certification by the veterinarian. Many puppies have problems with their knee caps, cataracts and other eye problems, heart murmurs and undescended testicles. They may also have personality problems and your veterinarian might have training in temperament evaluation.

VACCINATIONS

Most vaccinations are given by injection and should only be given by a vet. Both he and you should keep a record of the date

Your dog's routine will check-ups include having his eyes, ears and heartbeat checked—not unlike your own check-ups!

> **PET ADVANTAGES**
> If you do not intend to show or breed your new puppy, your veterinarian will recommend that you spay your female or neuter your male. Some people believe neutering leads to weight gain, but if you feed and exercise your dog properly, this is easily avoided. Spaying or neutering can actually have many positive outcomes, such as:
> - training becomes easier, as the dog focuses less on the urge to mate and more on you!
> - females are protected from unplanned pregnancy as well as ovarian and uterine cancers.
> - males are guarded from testicular tumors and have a reduced risk of developing prostate cancer.
>
> Talk to your vet regarding the right age to spay/neuter and other aspects of the procedure.

of the injection, the identification of the vaccine and the amount given. Some vets give a first vaccination at eight weeks, but most dog breeders prefer the course not to commence until about ten weeks because of the risk of interaction with the antibodies produced by the mother. The vaccination schedule is usually based on a 15-day cycle. You must take your vet's advice as to when to vaccinate, as this may differ according to the vaccine used.

HEALTH AND VACCINATION SCHEDULE

Age in Weeks:	3rd	6th	8th	10th	12th	14th	16th	20-24th
Worm Control	✔	✔	✔	✔	✔	✔	✔	✔
Neutering								✔
Heartworm		✔						✔
Parvovirus		✔		✔		✔		✔
Distemper			✔		✔		✔	
Hepatitis			✔		✔		✔	
Leptospirosis		✔		✔		✔		
Parainfluenza		✔		✔		✔		
Dental Examination			✔					✔
Complete Physical			✔					✔
Temperament Testing			✔					
Coronavirus					✔			
Kennel Cough		✔						
Hip Dysplasia							✔	
Rabies								✔

Vaccinations are not instantly effective. It takes about two weeks for the dog's immune system to develop antibodies. Most vaccinations require annual booster shots. Your veterinarian should guide you in this regard.

The usual vaccines contain immunizing doses of several different viruses such as distemper, parvovirus, parainfluenza and hepatitis. There are other vaccines available when the puppy is at risk. You should rely upon professional advice. This is especially true for the booster immunizations. Most vaccination programs require a booster when the puppy is a year old and once a year thereafter. In some cases, circumstances may require more or less frequent immunizations. Kennel cough, more formally known as tracheobronchitis, is immunized against with a vaccine

PUPPY WORM CONTROL

Caring for the puppy starts before the puppy is born by keeping the dam healthy and well-nourished. When the puppy is about three weeks old, he must start his disease-control regimen. The first treatments will be for worms. Most puppies have worms, even if they are tested negative for worms. The test essentially consists of checking stool specimens for the eggs of worms. The worms continually shed eggs, except during their dormant stage when they just rest in the tissues of the puppy. During this stage, they don't shed eggs and are not evident during a routine examination.

that is sprayed into the dog's nostrils. Kennel cough is usually included in routine vaccination, but it is often not as effective as the vaccines for other major diseases.

FIVE MONTHS TO ONE YEAR OF AGE
Unless you intend to breed or show your dog, neutering the puppy at six months of age is recommended; discuss this with your vet. A reputable breeder sells pups on the condition that any pups not intended or of sufficient quality for breeding and/or showing be neutered. Neutering/spaying has proven to be extremely beneficial to male

and female puppies, respectively. Besides eliminating the possibility of pregnancy, it inhibits (but does not prevent) breast cancer in bitches and prostate cancer in male dogs. Under no circumstances should a bitch be spayed prior to her first season.

Your vet should provide your puppy with a thorough dental evaluation at six months of age, ascertaining whether all the permanent teeth have erupted properly. A home dental-care regimen should be initiated at six months, including brushing weekly and providing good dental devices (such as hard

Disease	What is it?	What causes it?	Symptoms
Leptospirosis	Severe disease that affects the internal organs; can be spread to people.	A bacterium, which is often carried by rodents, that enters through mucous membranes and spreads quickly throughout the body.	Range from fever, vomiting and loss of appetite in less severe cases to shock, irreversible kidney damage and possibly death in most severe cases.
Rabies	Potentially deadly virus that infects warm-blooded mammals.	Bite from a carrier of the virus, mainly wild animals.	1st stage: dog exhibits change in behavior, fear. 2nd stage: dog's behavior becomes more aggressive. 3rd stage: loss of coordination, trouble with bodily functions.
Parvovirus	Highly contagious virus, potentially deadly.	Ingestion of the virus, which is usually spread through the feces of infected dogs.	Most common: severe diarrhea. Also vomiting, fatigue, lack of appetite.
Kennel cough	Contagious respiratory infection.	Combination of types of bacteria and virus. Most common: *Bordetella bronchiseptica* bacteria and parainfluenza virus.	Chronic cough.
Distemper	Disease primarily affecting respiratory and nervous system.	Virus that is related to the human measles virus.	Mild symptoms such as fever, lack of appetite and mucous secretion progress to evidence of brain damage, "hard pad."
Hepatitis	Virus primarily affecting the liver.	Canine adenovirus type I (CAV-1). Enters system when dog breathes in particles.	Lesser symptoms include listlessness, diarrhea, vomiting. More severe symptoms include "blue-eye" (clumps of virus in eye).
Coronavirus	Virus resulting in digestive problems.	Virus is spread through infected dog's feces.	Stomach upset evidenced by lack of appetite, vomiting, diarrhea.

DENTAL HEALTH

A dental examination is in order when the dog is between six months and one year of age so that any permanent teeth that have erupted incorrectly can be corrected. It is important to begin a tooth-brushing routine at home, using dental-care products made for dogs, including canine toothpaste and toothbrushes. Durable nylon and safe edible chews should be a part of your puppy's arsenal for good health, good teeth and pleasant breath. The vast majority of dogs three to four years old and older has diseases of the gums from lack of dental attention. Using the various types of dental chews can be very effective in controlling dental plaque.

plastic or nylon bones). Regular dental care promotes healthy teeth, fresh breath and a longer life.

Dogs Older Than One Year

Continue to visit the vet at least once a year. There is no such disease as "old age," but bodily functions do change with age. The eyes and ears are no longer as efficient. Liver, kidney and intestinal functions often decline. Proper dietary changes, recommended by your veterinarian, can make life more pleasant for your aging Labrador and you.

SKIN PROBLEMS IN LABRADOR RETRIEVERS

Veterinarians are consulted by dog owners for skin problems more than any other group of diseases or maladies. Dogs' skin is almost as sensitive as human skin and both suffer from almost the same maladies (though the occurrence of acne in most breeds of dog is rare). For this reason, veterinary dermatology has developed into a specialty practiced by many veterinarians.

Since many skin problems have visual symptoms which are almost identical, it requires the skill of an experienced veterinary dermatologist to identify and cure many of the more severe skin disorders. Pet shops sell many treatments for skin problems, but most of the treatments are simply directed at symptoms and not the underlying problem(s). Simply put, if your dog is suffering from a skin disorder, seek professional assistance as quickly as possible. As with all diseases, the earlier a

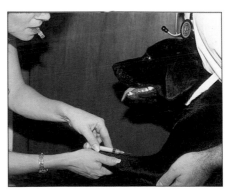

Your vet will oversee your Lab's vaccination booster program.

DETECTING BLOAT

Precautions against bloat/gastric torsion have been previously mentioned, and it is equally important to recognize the symptoms. It is necessary for your Lab to get immediate veterinary attention if you notice any of the following:

• Your dog's stomach starts to distend, ending up large and as tight as a football;
• Your dog is dribbling, as no saliva can be swallowed;
• Your dog makes frequent attempts to vomit but cannot bring anything up due to the stomach's being closed off;
• Your dog is distressed from pain;
• Your dog starts to suffer from clinical shock, meaning that there is not enough blood in the dog's circulation as the hard, dilated stomach stops the blood from returning to the heart to be pumped around the body. Clinical shock is indicated by pale gums and tongue, as they have been starved of blood. The shocked dog also has glazed, staring eyes.

You have minutes, yes *minutes,* to get your dog into surgery. If you see any of these symptoms at any time of the day or night, get to the vet immediately. Someone will have to phone and warn that you are on your way (which is a justification for the invention of the cellular phone!), so that they can be prepared to get your pet on the operating table.

problem is identified and treated, the more likely is a full recovery.

HEREDITARY SKIN DISORDERS
Veterinary dermatologists are currently researching a number of skin disorders that are believed to have a hereditary basis. These inherited diseases are transmitted by both parents, who appear (phenotypically) normal but have a recessive gene for the disease, meaning that they carry, but are not affected by, the disease. These diseases pose serious problems to breeders because in some instances there are no methods of identifying carriers. Often the secondary diseases associated with these skin conditions are even more debilitating than the skin disorders themselves, including cancers and respiratory problems.

Among the hereditary skin disorders for which the mode of inheritance is known are acrodermatitis, cutaneous asthenia (Ehlers-Danlos syndrome), sebaceous adenitis, cyclic hematopoiesis, dermatomyositis, IgA deficiency, color dilution alopecia and nodular dermatofibrosis. Some of these disorders are limited to one or two breeds, while others affect a large number of breeds. All inherited diseases must be diagnosed and treated by a veterinary specialist.

First Aid
at a Glance

Burns
Place the affected area under cool water;
use ice if only a small area is burnt.

Bee stings/Insect bites
Apply ice to relieve swelling;
antihistamine dosed properly.

Animal bites
Clean any bleeding area; apply pressure
until bleeding subsides; go to the vet.

Spider bites
Use cold compress and a pressurized
pack to inhibit venom's spreading.

Antifreeze poisoning
Immediately induce vomiting by using
hydrogen peroxide.

Fish hooks
Removal best handled by vet;
hook must be cut in order to remove.

Snake bites
Pack ice around bite; contact vet
quickly; identify snake for proper
antivenin.

Car accident
Move dog from roadway with blanket;
seek veterinary aid.

Shock
Calm the dog, keep him warm; seek
immediate veterinary help.

Nosebleed
Apply cold compress to the nose; apply
pressure to any visible abrasion.

Bleeding
Apply pressure above the area; treat
wound by applying a cotton pack.

Heat stroke
Submerge dog in cold bath; cool down
with fresh air and water; go to the vet.

Frostbite/Hypothermia
Warm the dog with a warm bath, electric
blankets or hot water bottles.

Abrasions
Clean the wound and clean out
thoroughly with fresh water;
apply antiseptic.

 *Remember: an injured dog may attempt to bite
a helping hand from fear and confusion.
Always muzzle the dog before trying to offer assistance.*

PARASITE BITES

Many of us are allergic to mosquito bites. The bites itch, erupt and may even become infected. Dogs have the same reaction to fleas, ticks and/or mites. When you feel the prick of the mosquito when it bites you, you have a chance to kill it with your hand. Unfortunately, when your dog is bitten by a flea, tick or mite, it can only scratch it away or bite it. By the time the dog has been bitten, the parasite has done some of its damage. It may also have laid eggs to cause further problems in the near future. The itching from parasite bites is

In between veterinary visits, check your Lab's skin and coat often for any signs of a problem. Any abnormalities should be brought to the attention of your vet.

probably due to the saliva injected into the site when the parasite sucks the dog's blood.

AIRBORNE ALLERGIES

Just as humans have hay fever, rose fever and other fevers with which they suffer during the pollinating season. Many dogs suffer the same allergies. So when the pollen count is high, your dog might suffer, but don't expect him to sneeze and have runny nose like a human would. Dogs react to pollen allergies the same way they react to fleas—they scratch and bite themselves. Labrador Retrievers are very susceptible to airborne pollen allergies.

Dogs, like humans, can be tested for allergens. Discuss the testing with your veterinary dermatologist.

ACRAL LICK GRANULOMA

Many large dogs have a very poorly understood syndrome

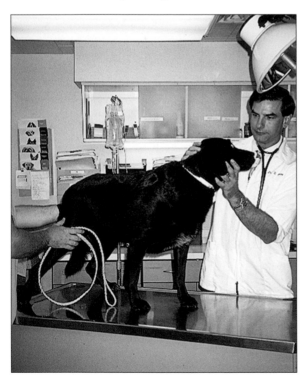

called acral lick granuloma. The manifestation of the problem is the dog's tireless attack at a specific area of the body, almost always the legs or paws. The dog licks so intensively that he removes the hair and skin, leaving an ugly, large wound. Tiny protuberances, which are outgrowths of new capillaries, bead on the surface of the wound. Owners who notice their dogs' biting and chewing at their extremities should have the vet determine the cause. If lick granuloma is identified, although there is no absolute cure, corticosteroids are the most common treatment.

SIMULATED MEDICAL CONDITION FOR EDUCATIONAL PURPOSES ONLY.

Acral lick syndrome results in a large open wound, a lick granuloma, usually on the dog's leg.

HOW TO PREVENT BLOAT

Research has confirmed that the structure of deep-chested breeds like the Labrador contributes to their predisposition to bloat, a condition in which the stomach twists on itself, cutting off the blood supply and increasing and trapping gas in the stomach. Nevertheless, there are several precautions that you can take to reduce the risk of this condition:

- Feed your dog twice daily rather than offer one big meal.
- Do not exercise your dog for at least one hour before and two hours after he has eaten.
- Make certain that your dog is calm and not overly excited while he is eating. It has been proven that nervous or overly excited dogs are more prone to develop bloat.
- Add a small portion of moist meat product to his dry food ration.
- Serve his meals and water in elevated bowl stands, which avoids the dog's craning his neck and swallowing air while eating and drinking.
- To prevent your dog from gobbling his food too quickly, and thereby swallowing air, put some large (unswallowable) toys into his bowl so that he will have to eat around them to get his food.
- Do not allow your dog to gulp water, especially at mealtimes.

It is essential to take these precautions with your Lab, as shock and resultant death can happen very quickly without immediate veterinary attention:

A male dog flea, *Ctenocephalides canis.*

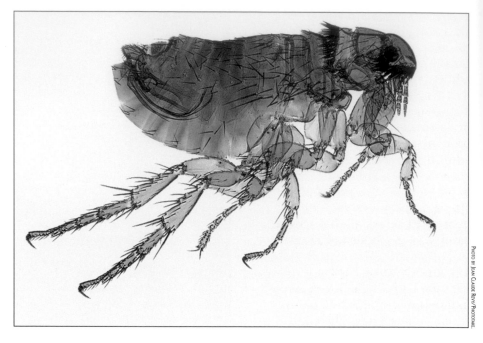

PHOTO BY JEAN CLAUDE REVY/PHOTOTAKE.

EXTERNAL PARASITES

FLEAS

Of all the problems to which dogs are prone, none is more well known and frustrating than fleas. Flea infestation is relatively simple to cure but difficult to prevent. Parasites that are harbored inside the body are a bit more difficult to eradicate but they are easier to control.

To control flea infestation, you have to understand the flea's life cycle. Fleas are often thought of as a summertime problem, but centrally heated homes have changed the patterns and fleas can be found at any time of the year. The most effective method of flea control is a two-stage approach: one stage to kill the adult fleas, and the other to control the development of pre-adult fleas. Unfortunately, no single active ingredient is effective against all stages of the life cycle.

FLEA KILLER CAUTION—"POISON"

Flea-killers are poisonous. You should not spray these toxic chemicals on areas of a dog's body that he licks, including his genitals and his face. Flea killers taken internally are a better answer, but check with your vet in case internal therapy is not advised for your dog.

LIFE CYCLE STAGES

During its life, a flea will pass through four life stages: egg, larva, pupa or nymph and adult. The adult stage is the most visible and irritating stage of the flea life cycle, and this is why the majority of flea-control products concentrate on this stage. The fact is that adult fleas account for only 1% of the total flea population, and the other 99% exist in pre-adult stages, i.e., eggs, larvae and nymphs. The pre-adult stages are barely visible to the naked eye.

THE LIFE CYCLE OF THE FLEA

Eggs are laid on the dog, usually in quantities of about 20 or 30, several times a day. The adult female flea must have a blood meal before each egg-laying session. When first laid, the eggs will cling to the dog's hair, as the eggs are still moist. However, they will quickly dry out and fall from the dog, especially if the dog moves around or scratches. Many eggs will fall off in the dog's favorite area or an area in which he spends a lot of time, such as his bed.

Once the eggs fall from the dog onto the carpet or furniture, they will hatch into larvae. This takes from one to ten days. Larvae are not particularly mobile and will usually travel only a few inches from where they hatch. However, they do have a tendency to move away from bright light and heavy

EN GARDE:
CATCHING FLEAS OFF GUARD!
Consider the following ways to arm yourself against fleas:
- Add a small amount of pennyroyal or eucalyptus oil to your dog's bath. These natural remedies repel fleas.
- Supplement your dog's food with fresh garlic (minced or grated) and a hearty amount of brewer's yeast, both of which ward off fleas.
- Use a flea comb on your dog daily. Submerge fleas in a cup of bleach to kill them quickly.
- Confine the dog to only a few rooms to limit the spread of fleas in the home.
- Vacuum daily...and get all of the crevices! Dispose of the bag every few days until the problem is under control.
- Wash your dog's bedding daily. Cover cushions where your dog sleeps with towels, and wash the towels often.

traffic—under furniture and behind doors are common places to find high quantities of flea larvae.

The flea larvae feed on dead organic matter, including adult flea feces, until they are ready to change into adult fleas. Fleas will usually remain as larvae for around seven days. After this period, the larvae will pupate into protective pupae. While inside the pupae, the larvae will undergo metamorphosis and change into adult fleas. This can take as little time as a few days, but the adult fleas can remain inside the pupae waiting to hatch for up to two years. The pupae are signaled to hatch by certain stimuli, such as physical pressure—the pupae's being stepped on, heat from an animal's lying on the pupae or increased carbon-dioxide levels and vibrations—indicating that a suitable host is available.

Once hatched, the adult flea must feed within a few days. Once the adult flea finds a host, it will not leave voluntarily. It only becomes dislodged by grooming or the host animal's scratching.

PHOTO BY DWIGHT R. KUHN

The adult flea will remain on the host for the duration of its life unless forcibly removed.

TREATING THE ENVIRONMENT AND THE DOG

Treating fleas should be a two-pronged attack. First, the environment needs to be treated; this includes carpets and furniture, especially the dog's bedding and areas underneath furniture. The environment should be treated with a household spray containing an Insect Growth Regulator (IGR) and an insecticide to kill the adult fleas. Most IGRs are effective against eggs and larvae; they actually mimic the fleas' own hormones and stop the eggs and larvae from developing into adult fleas. There are currently no treatments available to attack the pupa stage of the life cycle, so the adult insecticide is used to kill the newly hatched adult fleas before they find a host. Most IGRs are active for many months, while

A scanning electron micrograph of a dog or cat flea, *Ctenocephalides*, magnified more than 100x. This image has been colorized for effect.

S. E. M. BY DR DENNIS KUNKEL, UNIVERSITY OF HAWAII

THE LIFE CYCLE OF THE FLEA

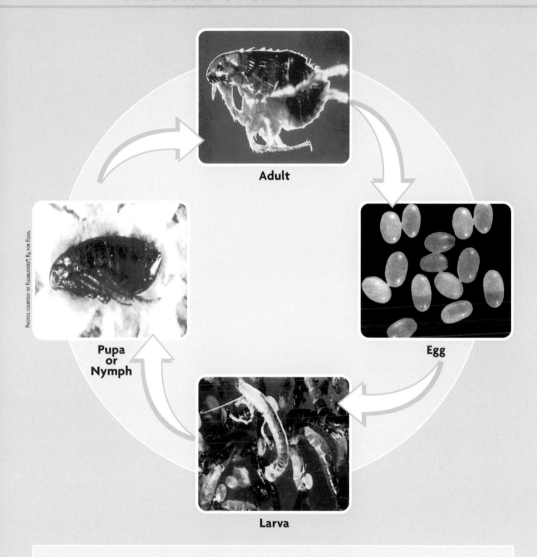

Adult

Egg

Larva

Pupa or Nymph

Fleas have been around for millions of years and have adapted to changing host animals. They are able to go through a complete life cycle in less than one month or they can extend their lives to almost two years by remaining as pupae or cocoons. They do not need blood or any other food for up to 20 months.

S. E. M. by Dr. Dennis Kunkel, University of Hawaii

INSECT GROWTH REGULATOR (IGR)

Two types of products should be used when treating fleas—a product to treat the pet and a product to treat the home. Adult fleas represent less than 1% of the flea population. The pre-adult fleas (eggs, larvae and pupae) represent more than 99% of the flea population and are found in the environment; it is in the case of pre-adult fleas that products containing an Insect Growth Regulator (IGR) should be used in the home.

IGRs are a new class of compounds used to prevent the development of insects. They do not kill the insect outright, but instead use the insect's biology against it to stop it from completing its growth. Products that contain methoprene are the world's first and leading IGRs. Used to control fleas and other insects, this type of IGR will stop flea larvae from developing and protect the house for up to seven months.

The American dog tick, *Dermacentor variabilis*, is probably the most common tick found on dogs. Look at the strength in its eight legs! No wonder it's hard to detach them.

adult insecticides are only active for a few days.

When treating with a household spray, it is a good idea to vacuum before applying the product. This stimulates as many pupae as possible to hatch into adult fleas. The vacuum cleaner should also be treated with an insecticide to prevent the eggs and larvae that have been collected in the vacuum bag from hatching.

The second stage of treatment is to apply an adult insecticide to the dog. Traditionally, this would be in the form of a collar or a spray, but more recent innovations include digestible insecticides that poison the fleas when they ingest the dog's blood. Alternatively, there are drops that, when placed on the back of the dog's neck, spread throughout the hair and skin to kill adult fleas.

TICKS

Though not as common as fleas, ticks are found all over the tropical and temperate world. They don't bite, like fleas; they harpoon. They dig their sharp proboscis (nose) into the dog's skin and drink the blood. Their

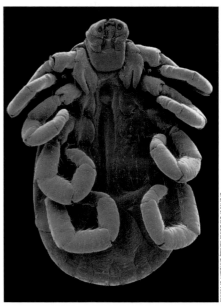

only food and drink is dog's blood. Dogs can get Lyme disease, Rocky Mountain spotted fever, tick bite paralysis and many other diseases from ticks. They may live where fleas are found and they like to hide in cracks or seams in walls. They are controlled the same way fleas are controlled.

The American dog tick, *Dermacentor variabilis*, may well be the most common dog tick in many geographical areas, especially those areas where the climate is hot and humid. Most dog ticks have life expectancies of a week to six months, depending upon climatic conditions. They can neither jump nor fly, but they can crawl slowly and can range up to 16 feet to reach a sleeping or unsuspecting dog.

MITES

Just as fleas and ticks can be problematic for your dog, mites can also lead to an itchy nuisance. Microscopic in size, mites are related to ticks and generally take up permanent residence on their host animal—in this case, your dog! The term *mange* refers to any infestation caused by one of the mighty mites, of which there are six varieties that concern dog owners.

Demodex mites cause a condition known as demodicosis

DEER-TICK CROSSING

The great outdoors may be fun for your dog, but it also is a home to dangerous ticks. Deer ticks carry a bacterium known as *Borrelia burgdorferi* and are most active in the autumn and spring. When infections are caught early, penicillin and tetracycline are effective antibiotics, but, if left untreated, the bacteria may cause neurological, kidney and cardiac problems as well as long-term trouble with walking and painful joints.

S.E.M. BY DR. ANDREW SPIELMAN/PHOTOTAKE.

PHOTO BY DR. DENNIS KUNKEL, UNIVERSITY OF HAWAII.

The head of an American dog tick, *Dermacentor variabilis*, enlarged and colorized for effect.

The mange mite, *Psoroptes bovis*, can infest cattle and other domestic animals.

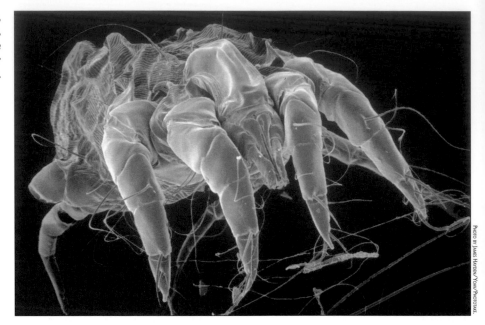

PHOTO BY JAMES HAYDEN/YOAV/PHOTOTAKE.

Human lice look like dog lice; the two are closely related.

PHOTO BY DWIGHT R. KUHN.

(sometimes called red mange or follicular mange), in which the mites live in the dog's hair follicles and sebaceous glands in larger-than-normal numbers. This type of mange is commonly passed from the dam to her puppies and usually shows up on the puppies' muzzles, though demodicosis is not transferable from one normal dog to another. Most dogs recover from this type of mange without any treatment, though topical therapies are commonly prescribed by the vet.

The *Cheyletiellosis* mite is the hook-mouthed culprit associated with "walking dandruff," a condition that affects dogs as well as cats and rabbits. This mite lives on the surface of the animal's skin and is readily transferable through direct or indirect contact with an affected animal. The dandruff is present in the form of scaly skin, which may or may not be itchy. If not treated, this mange can affect a whole kennel of dogs and can be spread to humans as well.

The *Sarcoptes* mite causes intense itching on the dog in the form of a condition known as scabies or sarcoptic mange. The cycle of the *Sarcoptes* mite lasts about three weeks, and the mites live in the top layer of the dog's skin (epidermis), preferably in areas with little hair. Scabies is highly contagious and can be passed to humans. Sometimes an allergic reaction to the mite worsens the severe itching associated with sarcoptic mange.

Ear mites, *Otodectes cynotis,* lead to otodectic mange, which most commonly affects the outer ear canal of the dog, though other areas can be affected as well. Dogs with ear-mite infestation commonly scratch at their ears, causing further irritation, and shake their heads. Dark brown droppings in the outer ear confirm the diagnosis. Your vet can prescribe a treatment to flush out the ears and kill any eggs in the ears. A complete month of treatment is necessary to cure the mange.

Two other mites, less common in dogs, include *Dermanyssus gallinac* (the poultry or red mite) and *Eutrombicula alfreddugesi* (the North American mite associated with trombiculidiasis or chigger infestation). The poultry mite frequently lives on chickens, but can transfer to dogs who spend time near farm animals. Chigger

---

DO NOT MIX
Never mix parasite control products without first consulting your vet. Some products can become toxic when combined with others and can cause fatal consequences.

NOT A DROP TO DRINK
Never allow your dog to swim in polluted water or public areas where water quality can be suspect. Even perfectly clear water can harbor parasites, many of which can cause serious to fatal illnesses in canines. Areas inhabited by waterfowl and other wildlife are especially dangerous.

---

infestation affects dogs in the Central U.S. who have exposure to woodlands. The types of mange caused by both of these mites are treatable by veterinarians.

INTERNAL PARASITES

Most animals—fishes, birds and mammals, including dogs and humans—have worms and other parasites that live inside their bodies. According to Dr. Herbert R. Axelrod, the fish pathologist, there are two kinds of parasites: dumb and smart. The smart parasites live in peaceful cooperation with their hosts (symbiosis), while the dumb parasites kill their hosts. Most worm infections are relatively easy to control. If they are not controlled, they weaken the host dog to the point that other medical problems occur, but they do not kill the host as dumb parasites would.

A brown dog tick, *Rhipicephalus sanguineus*, is an uncommon but annoying tick found on dogs.
PHOTO BY CAROLINA BIOLOGICAL SUPPLY/PHOTOTAKE.

PHOTO BY CAROLINA BIOLOGICAL SUPPLY/PHOTOTAKE

The roundworm *Rhabditis* can infect both dogs and humans.

ROUNDWORMS

Average-size dogs can pass 1,360,000 roundworm eggs every day. For example, if there were only 1 million dogs in the world, the world would be saturated with thousands of tons of dog feces. These feces would contain around 15,000,000,000 roundworm eggs.

Up to 31% of home yards and children's sand boxes in the US contain roundworm eggs.

Flushing dog's feces down the toilet is not a safe practice because the usual sewage treatments do not destroy roundworm eggs.

Infected puppies start shedding roundworm eggs at three weeks of age. They can be infected by their mother's milk.

The roundworm, *Ascaris lumbricoides.*

PHOTO BY DWIGHT R. KUHN

ROUNDWORMS

The roundworms that infect dogs are known scientifically as *Toxocara canis.* They live in the dog's intestines and shed eggs continually. It has been estimated that a dog produces about 6 or more ounces of feces every day. Each ounce of feces averages hundreds of thousands of roundworm eggs. There are no known areas in which dogs roam that do not contain roundworm eggs. The greatest danger of roundworms is that they infect people, too! It is wise to have your dog tested regularly for roundworms.

In young puppies, roundworms cause bloated bellies, diarrhea, coughing and vomiting, and are transmitted from the dam (through blood or milk). Affected puppies will not appear as animated as normal puppies. The worms appear spaghetti-like, measuring as long as 6 inches. Adult dogs can acquire roundworms through coprophagia (eating contaminated feces) or by killing rodents that carry roundworms.

Roundworm infection can kill puppies and cause severe problems in adults, as the hatched larvae travel to the lungs and trachea through the bloodstream. Cleanliness is the best preventative for roundworms. Always pick up after your dog and dispose of feces in appropriate receptacles.

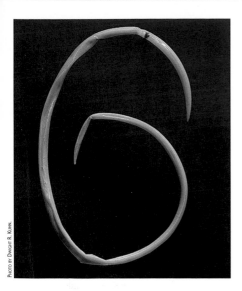

The hookworm, *Ancylostoma caninum.*

HOOKWORMS

In the United States, dog owners have to be concerned about four different species of hookworm, the most common and most serious of which is *Ancylostoma caninum,* which prefers warm climates. The others are *Ancylostoma braziliense, Ancylostoma tubaeforme* and *Uncinaria stenocephala,* the latter of which is a concern to dogs living in the Northern U.S. and Canada, as this species prefers cold climates. Hookworms are dangerous to humans as well as to dogs and cats, and can be the cause of severe anemia due to iron deficiency. The worm uses its teeth to attach itself to the dog's intestines and changes the site of its attachment about six times per day. Each time the worm repositions itself, the dog loses blood and can become anemic. *Ancylostoma caninum* is the most likely of the four species to cause anemia in the dog.

Symptoms of hookworm infection include dark stools, weight loss, general weakness, pale coloration and anemia, as well as possible skin problems. Fortunately, hookworms are easily purged from the affected dog with a number of medications that have proven effective. Discuss these with your veterinarian. Most heartworm preventatives include a hookworm insecticide as well.

Owners also must be aware that hookworms can infect humans, who can acquire the larvae through exposure to contaminated feces. Since the worms cannot complete their life cycle on a human, the worms simply infest the skin and cause irritation. This condition is known as cutaneous larva migrans syndrome. As a preventative, use disposable gloves or a "poop-scoop" to pick up your dog's droppings and prevent your dog (or neighborhood cats) from defecating in children's play areas.

The infective stage of the hookworm larva.

TAPEWORMS

Humans, rats, squirrels, foxes, coyotes, wolves and domestic dogs are all susceptible to tapeworm infection. Except in humans, tapeworms are usually not a fatal infection. Infected individuals can harbor 1000 parasitic worms.

Tapeworms, like some other types of worm, are hermaphroditic, meaning male and female in the same worm.

If dogs eat infected rats or mice, or anything else infected with tapeworm, they get the tapeworm disease. One month after attaching to a dog's intestine, the worm starts shedding eggs. These eggs are infective immediately. Infective eggs can live for a few months without a host animal.

The head and rostellum (the round prominence on the scolex) of a tapeworm, which infects dogs and humans.

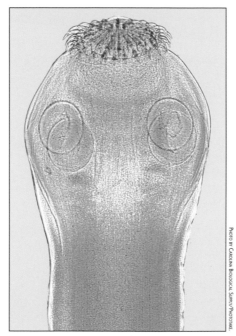

PHOTO BY CAROLINA BIOLOGICAL SUPPLY/PHOTOTAKE.

TAPEWORMS

There are many species of tapeworm, all of which are carried by fleas! The most common tapeworm affecting dogs is known as *Dipylidium caninum*. The dog eats the flea and starts the tapeworm cycle. Humans can also be infected with tapeworms—so don't eat fleas! Fleas are so small that your dog could pass them onto your hands, your plate or your food and thus make it possible for you to ingest a flea that is carrying tapeworm eggs.

While tapeworm infection is not life-threatening in dogs (smart parasite!), it can be the cause of a very serious liver disease for humans. About 50% of the humans infected with *Echinococcus multilocularis*, a type of tapeworm that causes alveolar hydatid, perish.

WHIPWORMS

In North America, whipworms are counted among the most common parasitic worms in dogs. The whipworm's scientific name is *Trichuris vulpis*. These worms attach themselves in the lower parts of the intestine, where they feed. Affected dogs may only experience upset tummies, colic and diarrhea. These worms, however, can live for months or years in the dog, beginning their larval stage in the small intestine, spending their adult stage in the large intestine and finally passing infective eggs through the dog's feces. The only way to detect whipworms is through a fecal examination, though this is not always foolproof. Treatment for whipworms is tricky, due to the worms' unusual life-cycle pattern, and very often dogs are reinfected due to exposure to infective eggs on the ground. The whipworm eggs can survive in the environment for as long as five years, thus cleaning up droppings in your own backyard as well as in public places is absolutely essential for sanitation purposes and the health of your dog and others.

THREADWORMS
Though less common than roundworms, hookworms and those previously mentioned, threadworms concern dog owners in the Southwestern U.S. and Gulf Coast area where the climate is hot and humid. Living in the small intestine of the dog, this worm measures a mere 2 millimeters and is round in shape. Like that of the whipworm, the threadworm's life cycle is very complex and the eggs and larvae are passed through the feces. A deadly disease in humans, *Strongyloides* readily infects people, and the handling of feces is the most common means of transmission. Threadworms are most often seen in young puppies; bloody diarrhea and pneumonia are symptoms. Sick puppies must be isolated and treated immediately; vets recommend a follow-up treatment one month later.

HEARTWORM PREVENTATIVES

There are many heartworm preventatives on the market, many of which are sold at your veterinarian's office. These products can be given daily or monthly, depending on the manufacturer's instructions. All of these preventatives contain chemical insecticides directed at killing heartworms, which leads to some controversy among dog owners. In effect, heartworm preventatives are necessary evils, though you should determine how necessary based on your pet's lifestyle. There is no doubt that heartworm is a dreadful disease that threatens the life of dogs. However, the likelihood of your dog's being bitten by an infected mosquito is slim in most places, and a mosquito-repellent (or an herbal remedy such as Wormwood or Black Walnut) is much safer for your dog and will not compromise his immune system (the way heartworm preventatives will). Should you decide to use the traditional preventative "medications," you can consider giving the pill every other or third month. Since the toxins in the pill will kill the heartworms at all stages of development, the pill would be effective in killing larvae, nymphs or adults and it takes four months for the larvae to reach the adult stage. Thus, there is no rationale to poisoning the dog's system on a monthly basis. Lastly, do not give the pill during the winter months since there are no mosquitoes around to pass on their infection, unless you live in a tropical environment.

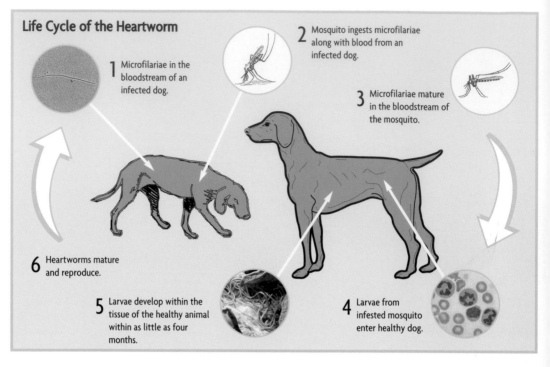

Life Cycle of the Heartworm

1 Microfilariae in the bloodstream of an infected dog.

2 Mosquito ingests microfilariae along with blood from an infected dog.

3 Microfilariae mature in the bloodstream of the mosquito.

4 Larvae from infested mosquito enter healthy dog.

5 Larvae develop within the tissue of the healthy animal within as little as four months.

6 Heartworms mature and reproduce.

HEARTWORMS

Heartworms are thin, extended worms up to 12 inches long, which live in a dog's heart and the major blood vessels surrounding it. Dogs may have up to 200 worms. Symptoms may be loss of energy, loss of appetite, coughing, the development of a pot belly and anemia.

Heartworms are transmitted by mosquitoes. The mosquito drinks the blood of an infected dog and takes in larvae with the blood. The larvae, called microfilariae, develop within the body of the mosquito and are passed on to the next dog bitten after the larvae mature. It takes two to three weeks for the larvae to develop to the infective stage within the body of the mosquito. Dogs are usually treated at about six weeks of age and maintained on a prophylactic dose given monthly.

Blood testing for heartworms is not necessarily indicative of how seriously your dog is infected. Although this is a dangerous disease, it is not easy for a dog to be infected. Discuss the various preventatives with your vet, as there are many different types now available. Together you can decide on a safe course of prevention for your dog.

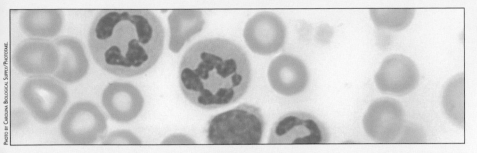

Magnified heartworm larvae, *Dirofilaria immitis.*

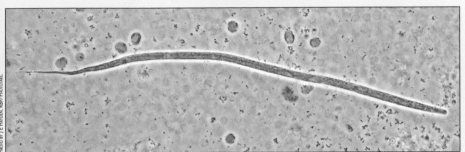

Heartworm, *Dirofilaria immitis.*

The heart of a dog infected with canine heartworm, *Dirofilaria immitis.*

BREED–SPECIFIC HEALTH CONCERNS

By and large, the Labrador Retriever is a healthy dog, blessed with a great enthusiasm for life, inclined toward activity and fresh air. While most Labradors love a romp through the meadow, beachfront or park with their owners, some Labradors tend to be sedentary, especially in their later years. Keeping the Labrador fit and trim is akin to keeping him healthy. Obesity can be a problem in any dog, purebred or mixed breed, just as it can be a problem with many humans. Since obesity can compromise the quality of your Labrador's life and shorten his years, it must be considered a serious threat. Studies show that obesity is the most prevalent nutrition-related problem of our pets and, among dogs, Labradors tip the scale! Veterinarians and nutrition specialists confirm that this disease has significant ties to the lifestyle of the owners. Over-weight owners, inclined to snack and share, tend to have overweight dogs. Labradors by definition are chow hounds, and nothing delights a Labrador more than chomping his way through a bag of chips! Don't judge your Labrador's happiness by his waist size—he'll be happier if he's trim and active, and he'll be around longer too.

The Labrador Retriever, like most other breeds of purebred dog, is disposed to a number of genetic diseases. Many veterinarians state that purebred dogs are much more inclined to hereditary disorders than are their mixed-breed counterparts.

Epilepsy (described as "idiopathic" or of unknown cause) runs in some lines of the Labrador, so only certain families are disposed. As in humans, epilepsy is characterized by recurrent seizures and is associated with the non-progressive brain disease. In Labradors, the disease occurs most frequently from the ages of six months to three years, and rarely ever over the age of five years. A dog undergoing a seizure usually loses consciousness and experiences stiffness in his limbs. A paddling movement followed by the dog crying, wetting himself, defecating and/or drooling describes the common occurrence. The dog becomes confused, drowsy and/or disoriented after the seizure.

TESTING FOR PROBLEMS
Purebred enthusiasts have become increasingly aware of congenital and hereditary problems of their dogs. Since breeds like the Labrador Retriever are blessed and cursed with such great popularity, many unsound dogs are bred each year. Responsible breeders test their dogs for the many conditions that affect Labrador Retrievers so that pet owners can have a healthy, sound dog that will live into its teens.

There are certain drugs available to control the frequency and intensity of the seizures. Since epilepsy is identified as a genetic/hereditary condition in Labrador Retrievers, no animals prone to seizures should be bred. Likewise, the siblings of affected animals should also be excluded from breeding programs. Spaying affected bitches will reduce seizures as well.

Two other conditions that affect the nervous systems of Labrador Retrievers include narcolespy and cataplexy. Narcolepsy is a sleeping disorder characterised by the animal's suddenly falling asleep with no signs of drowsiness, and frequently triggered by vigorous activity. It has been found to be of genetic cause in the Labrador Retriever and affects young pups between one to five months of age. Cataplexy is a similar disorder that involves the sleep-wake cycle's being altered. Both conditions are genetically based and therefore no Labradors with either condition should be bred.

Canine hip dysplasia bullies itself to the top of list of most breeds' hereditary problems, and the Labrador is no exception. Although not as badly affected as some other breeds, the incidence of hip dysplasia in Labradors is so high that it is the number-one genetic disease in the breed. Conscientious breeders have

reduced the incidence in the breed considerably, to nearly half of what it once was. Nevertheless, the incidence still lingers between 12 and 14 percent.

Hip dysplasia is basically a malformation of the hip joint. The disease grows worse as the dog ages, and all dysplastic dogs are born with normal hips. While many dogs are "susceptible" to hip dysplasia, based on genetic analysis, not all dogs develop the condition. Breeders ensure that the parents of the litter have been tested for hip dysplasia. This virtually ensures that your puppy will have strong, normal hips. Smart breeders know that hip dysplasia can be "instigated" by the environment; thus, they line their whelping boxes with slip-proof materials (that the puppies can't eat). Studies have proven that puppies who are forced to slip and slide on hard surfaces in their whelping boxes have a higher incidence of hip dysplasia. Pet people as well as show people and field people have to be

Unrestrained exercise such as jumping can contribute to dysplastic changes in dogs predisposed to the condition.

The more attention you pay to your Lab's health care, the longer and happier life you will have with your canine friend.

concerned about hip dysplasia. In its most severe form, your Labrador will be unable to run and play. Hip dysplasia can grossly compromise the life of your Labrador.

After the age of 16 weeks, your Labrador pup can be tested by a veterinarian. Owners can also lessen the possibility of the onset of dysplasia by controlling the dog's environment and diet. Breeders recommend feeding a moderate amount of protein and avoiding any foods that are high in calories. Avoid nutritional supplements and feed for a specified interval. Regulate the amount and kind of exercise that your Labrador gets. The breed tends to be somewhat overexuberant in play, so vigorous roughhousing should be avoided for fear of injuring the dog's hips and elbows.

Some Labradors with hip dysplasia experience great discomfort, while others seem only mildly distressed. The ultimate concern of owners is that hip dysplasia contributes to the onset of degenerative joint diseases, such as osteoarthritis, which can render the joint useless.

Predominantly affecting young dogs, elbow dysplasia refers to a system of disorders of the elbow joint. Affected dogs experience sudden lameness. Arthritis usually develops in the elbow joint. Initial problems usually manifest themselves when the puppy is four to seven months old. Like hip dysplasia, elbow dysplasia is a congenital defect and no affected animals should be bred. Considering that elbow dysplasia is less understood and its mode of passing more complicated, it's even more vital that Labradors with elbow dysplasia be excluded from breeding programs. The disease has been reported in males nearly 50% more often than in females. Owners are recommended to follow the same preventative recommendations as for hip dysplasia.

Osteochondrosis affects the cartilage of Labrador Retrievers and other large-breed dogs. The condition is characterized by improperly formed cartilage that forms thick patches on the dog's bones. This cartilage is not firmly attached to the dog's bones and causes inflammation, at which time it is referred to as osteochondritis dissccans (OCD). It can appear in the stifle joint, shoulder, elbow or hock, and most often affects young dogs, usually less than seven months old. Due to the inability of the affected dog to support his own weight, lameness, usually initially in one leg only, is the first sign. In Labradors, males are more commonly affected than females.

A common blood disorder, affecting many purebred dogs, is called von Willebrand's disease. This inherited bleeding disorder, which can be passed by one or both parents, is characterized by a variable lack of blood clotting. It is advisable for all Labrador owners to have their vets perform a test for the level of vWD factor in their dogs' blood. The clotting factor can range from very low (10 to 15%) to high (70% or more); the lower the factor, the more severe the case. Be sure to have your Labrador checked before a spaying or neutering operation. Dogs with less than 30% clotting factor may have gone undetected until spaying or neutering, and then are noticed when uncontrollable bleeding or the formation of hematomas occurs during the operation. Discuss vWD with your vet to learn more about the disease.

Eye problems have become fairly prevalent in the Labrador Retriever, including progressive retinal atrophy (PRA), cataracts, retinal dysplasia, ectropion, entropion, distichiasis and others. PRA causes blindness in Labrador Retrievers, affecting the retina and progressively deteriorating it. There is no cure, and blindness always results eventually. Breeding animals should be certified as free of of PRA before being included in a program.

Cataracts, unlike PRA, rarely cause blindness in the Labrador Retriever. A cataract is visualized as a cloudiness over the lens of the eye. Veterinary science has made it possible to operate to remove a cataract, even though vision is not affected. Animals with cataracts should not be bred, since cataracts are hereditary. Likewise, Labradors suffering from retinal dysplasia, causing blindness in young dogs, should not be bred.

Since we have discussed the problem of obesity in Labradors, we should also discuss the condition known as hypothyroidism. Hypothyroidism, affecting the hormonal system of dogs, is often confused with obesity, though there is no link in reality. Many Labrador owners have concluded that, since the only dogs ever detected with hypothyroidism have been greatly overweight, there is a correspondence between the two. Hypothyroidism simply means that the dog is not producing enough thyroid hormones. This disease begins to develop between the ages of one and three, though most owners aren't aware of it until much later. Affected dogs appear lackluster and without energy; only a very small percentage of dogs suffer from obesity. Many dogs lose their fur. Diagnosis is difficult and complicated, though the treatment is affordable and very successful. Affected dogs should never be used for breeding.

Some Labradors develop liver disease as young adults. Liver disease in Labradors has been compared to Wilson's disease in humans. A test for copper toxicity can reveal a carrier of this hereditary liver disease, which affects a number of breeds and is a major problem in the Bedlington Terrier. Affected dogs and carriers should not be bred.

DO YOU KNOW ABOUT HIP DYSPLASIA?

Hip dysplasia is a fairly common condition found in Labrador Retrievers, as well as other breeds. When a dog has hip dysplasia, its hind leg has an incorrectly formed hip joint. By constant use of the hip joint, it becomes more and more loose, wears abnormally and may become arthritic.

Hip dysplasia can only be confirmed with an x-ray, but certain symptoms may indicate a problem. Your Labrador Retriever may have a hip dysplasia problem if he walks in a peculiar manner, hops instead of smoothly running, uses his hind legs in unison (to keep the pressure off the weak joint), has trouble getting up from a prone position and always sits with both legs together on one side of his body.

As the dog matures, he may adapt well to life with a bad hip, but in a few years the arthritis develops and many Labrador Retrievers with hip dysplasia become cripples.

Hip dysplasia is considered an inherited disease and can usually be diagnosed when the dog is under a year old, although the dog cannot be certified as dysplasia-free until after two years of age. Some experts claim that a special diet might help your puppy outgrow the bad hip, but the usual treatments are surgical: the removal of the pectineus muscle, the removal of the round part of the femur, reconstructing the pelvis and replacing the hip with an artificial one. All of these surgical interventions are expensive, but they are usually very successful. Follow the advice of your veterinarian.

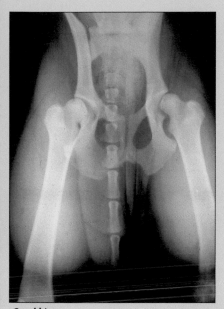

Good hips.

Compare the two hip joints and you'll understand dysplasia. Hip dysplasia is a badly worn hip joint caused by improper fit of the bone into the socket. It is easily the most common hip problem in Labrador Retrievers.

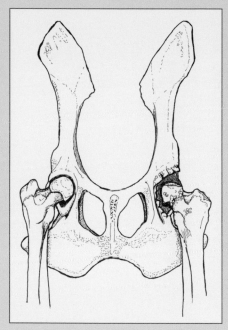

The healthy hip joint on the left and the unhealthy hip joint on the right.

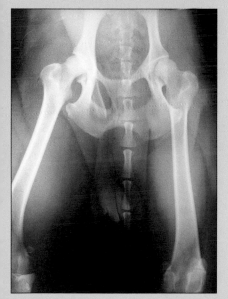

Moderate dysplasia.

YOUR SENIOR
LABRADOR RETRIEVER

SENIOR SIGNS

An old dog starts to show one or more of the following symptoms:

- The hair on the face and paws starts to turn gray. The color breakdown usually starts around the eyes and mouth.
- Sleep patterns are deeper and longer, and the old dog is harder to awaken.
- Food intake diminishes.
- Responses to calls, whistles and other signals are ignored more and more.
- Eye contact does not evoke tail wagging (assuming it once did).

The term *old* is a qualitative term. For dogs, as well as for their masters, old is relative. Certainly we can all distinguish between a puppy Labrador and an adult Labrador. Puppies and young dogs like to play with children. Children's natural exuberance is a good match for the seemingly endless energy of young dogs. When dogs grow older and cease their interaction with children, they are often thought of as being too old to keep pace with the children. On the other hand, if a Labrador is only exposed to people with quieter lifestyles, his life will normally be less active and the decrease in his activity level as he ages will not be as obvious.

If people live to be 100 years old, dogs live to be 20 years old. While this might seem like a good rule of thumb, it is very inaccurate. When trying to compare dog years to human years, you cannot make a generalization about all dogs. Labrador owners are lucky in that they have a long-lived breed, with the average lifespan being around 13 years.

Dogs in general are considered physically mature at three years of age (or earlier), but can reproduce even earlier. So the first three years of a dog's life are like seven times that of comparable humans. That means a 3-year-old dog is like a 21-year-old human. As the curve of comparison shows, there is no hard and fast rule for comparing dog and human ages. Small breeds tend to live longer than large breeds, some breeds' adolescent periods last longer than others' and some breeds experience rapid periods of growth.

CARE OF THE SENIOR DOG

Most veterinarians and behaviorists use the seven-year mark as the time to consider a dog a senior. This term does not imply that the dog is geriatric and has begun to fail in mind and body. Aging is essentially a slowing process. By treating the seven-year-old dog as a senior, owners are able to implement certain therapeutic and preventative medical strategies with the help of their vets.

A special-care program should include at least two veterinary visits per year and screening sessions to determine the dog's health status, as well as nutritional counseling. Veterinarians determine a senior dog's health status through a blood smear for a complete blood count, serum chemistry profile with electrolytes, urinalysis, blood pressure check, electrocardiogram, ocular

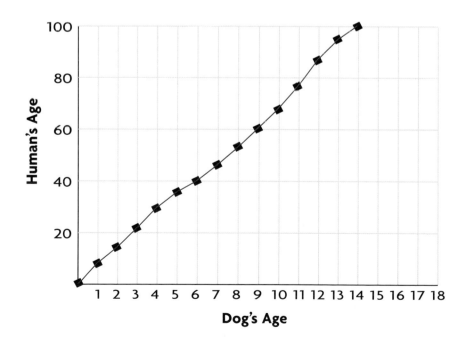

tonometry (pressure on the eyeball) and dental prophylaxis.

Such an extensive program for senior dogs is well advised before owners start to see the obvious physical signs of aging, such as slower and inhibited movement, graying, increased sleep/nap periods and disinterest in play and other activity. This preventative program promises a longer, healthier life for the aging dog.

There are also some behavioral changes and problems related to aging dogs. Dogs suffering from hearing or vision loss, dental discomfort or arthritis can become aggressive. Likewise, the near-deaf and/or blind dog may be startled more easily and react in an unexpectedly aggressive manner. Potty accidents are associated with loss of mobility, kidney problems and loss of sphincter control as well as plaque accumulation, physiological brain changes and reactions to medications. Older

Graying is a telltale sign of aging in dogs, too! Gray hairs on the muzzle are a sure indication of the dog's getting older.

NOTICING THE SYMPTOMS

The symptoms listed below are symptoms that gradually appear and become more noticeable. They are not life-threatening; however, the symptoms below are to be taken very seriously and warrant a discussion with your veterinarian:

- Your dog cries and whimpers when he moves, and he stops running completely.
- Convulsions start or become more serious and frequent. The usual convulsion (spasm) is when the dog stiffens and starts to tremble, being unable or unwilling to move. The seizure usually lasts for 5 to 30 minutes.
- Your dog drinks more water and urinates more frequently. Wetting and bowel accidents take place indoors without warning.
- Vomiting becomes more and more frequent.

dogs can suffer from separation anxiety, which can lead to excessive barking, whining, housesoiling and destructive behavior. Aging dogs may become fearful of everyday sounds. Some may have difficulty sleeping, due to discomfort, the need for frequent toilet visits and the like.

Owners should avoid spoiling the older dog with too many fatty treats. Obesity is a common problem in older dogs and subtracts years from their lives. Keep the senior dog as trim as possible, since excessive weight puts additional stress on the body's vital organs. Some breeders recommend supplementing the diet with foods high in fiber and lower in calories. Adding fresh vegetables and marrow broth to the senior's diet makes a tasty, low-calorie, low-fat supplement. Vets also offer specialty diets for senior dogs that are worth exploring.

Your dog, as he nears his twilight years, needs your patience and good care more than ever. Never punish an older dog for an accident or abnormal behavior. For all the years of love, protection and companionship that your dog has provided, he deserves special attention and courtesies. The older dog may need to relieve himself at 3 a.m. because he can no longer hold it for eight hours. Older dogs may not be able to remain crated for more than two or three hours. It may be time to give up a sofa or chair to your old friend. Although he may not seem as enthusiastic

about your attention and petting, he does appreciate the considerations you offer as he gets older.

WHEN THE TIME COMES

You are never fully prepared to make a rational decision about putting your dog to sleep. It is very obvious that you love your Labrador Retriever or you would not be reading this book. Putting a beloved dog to sleep is extremely difficult. It is a decision that must be made with your veterinarian. You are usually forced to make the decision when your dog experiences one or more life-threatening symptoms that have become serious enough for you to seek veterinary assistance.

WHAT IS EUTHANASIA?

Euthanasia derives from the Greek, meaning *good death*. In other words, it means the planned, painless killing of a dog suffering from a painful, incurable condition, or who is so aged that he cannot walk, see, eat or control

Pet cemeteries cater to pet lovers who wish to memorialize their pets in this manner.

his excretory functions. Euthanasia is usually accomplished by injection with an overdose of anesthesia or a barbiturate. Aside from the prick of the needle, the experience is usually painless.

MAKING THE DECISION

The decision to euthanize your dog is never easy. The days during which the dog becomes ill and the end occurs can be unusually stressful for you. If this is your first experience with the death of a loved one, you may need the comfort dictated by your religious beliefs. If you are the head of the family and have children, you should have involved them in the decision of putting your Labrador to sleep. Usually your dog can be maintained on drugs for a few days in order to give you ample time to make a decision. During this time, talking with members of your family or with people who have lived through the same experience can help.

THE FINAL RESTING PLACE

Dogs can have some of the same privileges as humans. The remains of your beloved dog can be buried in a pet cemetery, which is generally expensive. If your dog has died at home, he can be buried in your yard in a suitable spot marked by a stone, flowers or a newly planted tree. Alternatively, your dog can be cremated individually and the

ashes returned to you. A less expensive option is mass cremation, although, of course, the ashes cannot then be returned. Vets can usually help you locate a pet cemetery or arrange the cremation on your behalf. The cost of these options should always be discussed frankly and openly with your veterinarian.

GETTING ANOTHER DOG?

The grief of losing your beloved dog will be as lasting as the grief of losing a human friend or relative. In most cases, if your dog died of old age (if there is such a thing), it had slowed down considerably. Do you want a new Labrador puppy to replace it? Or are you better off finding a more mature Labrador, say two to three years of age, which will usually be house-trained and will have an already developed personality. In this case, you can find out if you like each other after a few hours of being together.

The decision is, of course, your own. Do you want another Labrador or perhaps a different breed so as to avoid comparison with your beloved friend? Most people usually buy the same breed because they know (and love) the characteristics of that breed. Then, too, they often know people who have the same breed and perhaps a breeder that they respect expects a litter soon. What could be better?

CDS: COGNITIVE DYSFUNCTION SYNDROME
"Old-Dog Syndrome"

There are many ways to evaluate old-dog syndrome. Veterinarians have defined CDS (cognitive dysfunction syndrome) as the gradual deterioration of cognitive abilities. These are indicated by changes in the dog's behavior. When a dog changes its routine response, and maladies have been eliminated as the cause of these behavioral changes, then CDS is the usual diagnosis.

More than half the dogs over 8 years old suffer some form of CDS. The older the dog, the more chance it has of suffering from CDS. In humans, doctors often dismiss these behavioral changes as part of "winding down."

There are four major signs of CDS: frequent housebreaking accidents inside the home, sleeping much more or much less than normal, acting confused and failing to respond to social stimuli.

SYMPTOMS OF CDS

FREQUENT HOUSEBREAKING ACCIDENTS
- *Urinates in the house.*
- *Defecates in the house.*
- *Doesn't signal that he wants to go out.*

SLEEP PATTERNS
- *Awakens more slowly.*
- *Sleeps more than normal during the day.*
- *Sleeps less during the night.*

CONFUSION
- *Walks around listlessly and without a destination goal.*
- *Goes outside and just stands there.*
- *Appears confused with a faraway look in his eyes.*
- *Hides more often.*
- *Doesn't recognize friends.*
- *Doesn't come when called.*

FAILURE TO RESPOND TO SOCIAL STIMULI
- *Comes to people less frequently, whether called or not.*
- *Doesn't tolerate petting for more than a short time.*
- *Doesn't come to the door when you return home from work.*

SHOWING YOUR
LABRADOR RETRIEVER

Both dog and handler must learn the ins and outs of ring procedure. This experience and knowledge is gained with time, practice and entering shows.

When you purchase your Labrador Retriever, you will make it clear to the breeder if you hope to be buying an Labrador with show prospects. No reputable breeder will sell you a young puppy and tell you that it is *definitely* of show quality, for so much can go wrong during the early months of a puppy's development. If you plan to show, what you will hopefully have acquired is a puppy with "show potential."

To the novice, exhibiting a Labrador Retriever in the show ring may look easy, but it takes a lot of hard work and devotion to do top winning. The first concept that the novice learns is that each dog first competes against members of its own breed. Once the judge has selected the best member of each breed (Best of Breed), provided that the show is

judged on a Group system, that chosen dog will compete with other dogs in its group. Finally, the dogs chosen first in each group will compete for Best in Show.

The second concept that you must understand is that the dogs are not actually compared against one another. The judge compares each dog against its breed standard, the written description of the ideal specimen that is approved by the American Kennel Club (AKC). Breeders attempt to get as close to this ideal as possible with every litter, but theoretically the "perfect" dog is so elusive that it is impossible.

AKC GROUPS
For showing purposes, the American Kennel Club divides its recognized breeds into seven groups: Sporting Dogs, Hounds, Working Dogs, Terriers, Toys, Non-Sporting Dogs and Herding Dogs.

If you are interested in exploring the world of dog showing, your best bet is to join your local breed club or the national parent club, which is the Labrador Retriever Club, Inc. These clubs often host both regional and national specialties, shows only for Labrador Retrievers, which can include conformation as well as obedience and field trials. Even if you have no intention of competing with your Lab, a specialty is a like a festival for lovers of the breed who congregate to share their favorite topic: Labrador Retrievers! Clubs also send out newsletters, and some organize training days and seminars in order that people may learn more about their chosen breed. To locate the breed club closest to you, contact American Kennel Club, which furnishes the rules and regulations for all of these events plus general dog registration and other basic requirements of dog ownership.

In the U.S., the American Kennel Club offers three kinds of conformation shows: an all-breed show (for all AKC-recognized breeds), a specialty show (for one breed only, usually sponsored by the parent club) and a Group show (for all breeds in the Group).

For a dog to become an AKC champion of record, the dog must accumulate 15 points at the shows from at least three different judges, including two "majors." A

What an exciting experience it is for dog and handler to share the excitement of bringing home a ribbon!

"major" is defined as a three-, four- or five-point win, and the number of points per win is determined on the number of dogs entered in the show on the day. Depending on the breed, the number of points that are awarded varies. In a breed as popular as the Labrador Retriever, more dogs are needed to rack up the points. At any dog show, only one dog and one bitch of each breed can win points.

Dog showing does not offer "co-ed" classes. Dogs and bitches never compete against each other in the classes. Non-champion dogs are called "class dogs" because they compete in one of five classes. Dogs are entered in a particular class depending on its age and previous show wins. To begin, there is the Puppy Class (for 6- to 9-month-olds and for 9- to 12-month-olds); followed by the Novice Class (for dogs that have not won any first prizes except in the Puppy Class or three first prizes in the Novice Class and have not accumulated any points toward their champion title); the Bred-by Exhibitor Class (for dogs handled by their breeders or one of the breeder's immediate family); American-bred Class (for dogs bred in the U.S.A.!); and the Open Class (for any dog that is not a champion).

The judge at the show begins judging the Puppy Class, first dogs and then bitches, and proceeds through the classes. The judge places his winners first through fourth in each class. In the Winners Class, the first-place winners of each class compete with one another to determine Winners Dog and Winners Bitch. The judge also places a Reserve Winners Dog and Reserve Winners Bitch, which could be awarded the points in the case of a disqualification. The Winners Dog and Winners Bitch are the two that are awarded the points for the breed, then compete with any champions

Each dog stands at attention, looking his best, as the judge moves down the line in her evaluation.

GETTING INVOLVED IN THE DOG SPORT

To find out about dog shows and trials in your area, you can subscribe to the American Kennel Club's monthly magazine, the *American Kennel Gazette* and the accompanying *Events Calendar.* You can also look in your local newspaper for advertisements for dog shows in your area or go on the Internet to the AKC's website, www.akc.org.

of record entered in the show. The judge reviews the Winners Dog, Winners Bitch and all the other champions to select his Best of Breed. The Best of Winners is selected between the Winners Dog and Winners Bitch. Were one of these two to be selected Best of Breed, it would automatically be named Best of Winners as well. Finally the judge selects his Best of Opposite Sex to the Best of Breed winner.

At a Group show or all-breed show, the Best of Breed winners from each breed then compete against one another for Group One through Group Four. The judge compares each Best of Breed to its breed standard, and the dog that most closely lives up to the ideal for its breed is selected as Group One. Finally, all seven group winners (from the Sporting Group, Toy Group, Hound Group, etc.) compete for Best in Show.

If your Labrador Retriever is six months of age or older and registered with the AKC, you can enter him a dog show where the breed is offered classes. Provided that your Labrador does not have a disqualifying fault, he can compete. Only unaltered dogs can be entered in a dog show, so if you have spayed or neutered your Labrador, you cannot compete in conformation shows. The reason for this is simple. Dog shows are the main forum to prove which representatives in a breed are worthy of being bred. Only dogs that have achieved champi-onships—the AKC "seal of approval" for quality in pure-bred dogs—should be bred. Altered dogs, however, can participate in other AKC events such as obedience trials and the Canine Good Citizen program.

Before you actually step into the ring, you would be well advised to sit back and observe the judge's ring procedure. If it is your first time in the ring, do not be over-anxious and run to the front of the line. It is much better to stand back and study how the exhibitor in front of you is performing. The judge asks each handler to "stack" the dog, hopefully showing the dog off to his best advantage. The judge will observe the dog from a distance and from different angles, and approach the dog to check his teeth, overall structure, alertness

Correct movement is imperative in a Sporting breed like the Lab, as it indicates that the dog would be able to perform his intended functions in the field.

and muscle tone, as well as consider how well the dog "conforms" to the standard. Most importantly, the judge will have the exhibitor move the dog around the ring in some pattern that he should specify (another advantage to not going first, but always listen since some judges change their directions—and the judge is always right!). Finally, the judge will give the dog one last look before moving on to the next exhibitor.

If you are not in the top four in your class at your first show, do not be discouraged. Be patient and consistent, and you may eventually find yourself in a winning line-up. Remember that the winners were once in your shoes and have devoted many hours and much money to earn the placement. If you find that your dog is losing every time and never getting a nod, it may be time to consider a different dog sport or to just enjoy your Lab as a pet. Parent clubs offer other events, such as agility, tracking,

Contending dogs are thoroughly examined by the judges and the dogs must readily tolerate such examinations.

obedience, instinct tests and more, which may be of interest to the owner of a well-trained Labrador Retriever.

OBEDIENCE TRIALS

Obedience trials in the U.S. trace back to the early 1930s when organized obedience training was developed to demonstrate how well dog and owner could work together. The pioneer of obedience trials is Mrs. Helen Whitehouse Walker, a Standard Poodle fancier, who designed a series of exercises after the Associated Sheep, Police, Army Dog Society of Great Britain. In the first obedience trial, held in 1933, the winning dog was none other than a Labrador Retriever! Since the days of Mrs. Walker, obedience trials have grown by leaps and bounds, and today there are over 2,000 trials held in the US every year, with more than 100,000 dogs competing. Any registered AKC dog can enter an obedience trial,

regardless of conformational disqualifications or neutering.

Obedience trials are divided into three levels of progressive difficulty. At the first level, the Novice, dogs compete for the title Companion Dog (CD); at the intermediate level, the Open, dogs compete for the title Companion Dog Excellent (CDX); and at the advanced level, dogs compete for the title Utility Dog (UD). A perfect score at any level is 200, and a dog must score 170 or better to earn a "leg," of which three are needed to earn the title. To earn points, the dog must score more than 50% of the available points in each exercise; the possible points range from 20 to 40.

Once a dog has earned the UD title, he can compete with other proven obedience dogs for the coveted title of Utility Dog Excellent (UDX), which requires that the dog win "legs" in ten shows. Utility Dogs who earn "legs" in Open B and Utility B earn points toward their Obedience Trial Champion title. To become an OTCh., a dog needs to earn 100 points, which requires three first places in Open B and Utility under three different judges. The Grand Prix of obedience trials, the AKC National Obedience Invitational gives qualifying Utility Dogs the chance to win the newest and highest title: National Obedience Champion (NOC).

AGILITY TRIALS

Having had its origins in the U.K. back in 1977, AKC agility had its official beginning in the U.S. in August 1994, when the first licensed agility trials were held. The AKC allows all registered breeds (including Miscellaneous Class breeds) to participate, providing the dog is 12 months of age or older. Agility is designed so that the handler demonstrates how well the dog can work at his side. The handler directs his dog over an obstacle course that includes jumps as well as tires, the dog walk, weave poles, pipe tunnels, collapsed tunnels, etc. The handler gives verbal and hand signals to guide the dog through the course.

The first organization to promote agility trials in the U.S. was the United States Dog Agility Association, Inc. (USDAA), which was established in 1986 and spawned numerous member clubs around the country. Both the USDAA and the AKC offers titles to winning dogs.

Agility is great fun for dog and owner with many rewards for everyone involved. Interested owners should join a training club that has obstacles and experienced agility handlers who can introduce you and your dog to the "ropes" (and tires, tunnels, etc.).

TRACKING

Any dog is capable of tracking, using its nose to follow a trail.

Tracking tests are exciting and competitive ways to test your Labrador Retriever's ability to search and rescue. The AKC started tracking tests in 1937, when the first AKC-licensed test took place as part of the Utility level at an obedience trial. Ten years later in 1947, the AKC offered the first title, Tracking Dog (TD). It was not until 1980 that the AKC added the Tracking Dog Excellent title (TDX), which was followed by the Versatile Surface Tracking title (VST) in 1995. The title Champion Tracker (CT) is awarded to a dog who has earned all three titles.

FIELD TRIALS

Field trials are offered to the retrievers, pointers and spaniel breeds of the Sporting Group as well as to the Beagles, Dachshunds and Bassets of the Hound Group.

The Lab is capable of breezing through the agility obstacles with speed, grace and accuracy.

The first AKC-licensed field trial was held in December of 1931, and Labradors have been competing ever since. The events vary depending on the type of dog, but in all trials dogs compete against one another for placement and for points toward their Field Champion (FC) titles. Dogs that earn championships in both field trials and conformation shows attain Dual Champion status; the first Labrador to become a Dual Champion in the US was Michael of Glenmere, earning both champion titles in 1941.

Retriever field trials, designed to simulate "an ordinary day's shoot," are popular and likely the most demanding of these trials. Dogs are tested both on land and water. Difficulty levels are based on the number of birds downed as well as the number of "blind retrieves" (where a bird is placed away from the view of the dog and the handler directs the dog by the use of hand signals and verbal commands). Every field trial includes four stakes of increasing levels of difficulty. Each stake is judged by a team of two judges who look for many natural abilities including steadiness, courage, style, control and training.

HUNTING TESTS

Hunting tests are not competitive like field trials, and participating dogs are judged against a standard like in a conformation show. The first hunting tests were devised by the North American Hunting Retriever Association (NAHRA) as an alternative to field trials for retriever owners to appreciate their dogs' natural innate ability in the field without the expense and pressure of a formal field trial. The intent of hunting tests is the same as that of field trials, to test the dog's ability in a simulated hunting scenario.

The AKC instituted its hunting tests in June 1985 and popularity has grown tremendously. In addition to the AKC, the United Kennel Club also offers hunting tests through its affiliate club, the Hunting Retriever Club, Inc. (HRC), which began the tests in 1984.

INFORMATION ON CLUBS

You can get information about dog shows from the national kennel clubs:

American Kennel Club
5580 Centerview Dr., Raleigh, NC 27606-3390
www.akc.org

United Kennel Club
100 E. Kilgore Road, Kalamazoo, MI 49002
www.ukcdogs.com

Canadian Kennel Club
89 Skyway Ave., Suite 100, Etobicoke, Ontario
M9W 6R4 Canada
www.ckc.ca

The Kennel Club
1-5 Clarges St., Piccadilly, London W1Y 8AB, UK
www.the-kennel-club.org.uk

THE BEHAVIOR OF YOUR
LABRADOR RETRIEVER

As a Labrador Retriever owner, you have selected your dog so that you and your loved ones can have a companion, a protector, a friend and a four-legged family member. You invest time, money and effort to care for and train the family's new charge. Of course, this chosen canine behaves perfectly! Well, perfectly like a *dog*.

THINK LIKE A DOG

Dogs do not think like humans, nor do humans think like dogs, though we try. Unfortunately, a dog is incapable of figuring out how humans think, so the responsibility falls on the owner to adopt a proper canine mindset. Dogs cannot rationalize, and dogs exist in the present moment. Many a dog owner makes the mistake in training of thinking that he can reprimand his dog for something the dog did a while ago. Basically, you cannot even reprimand a dog for something he did 20 seconds ago! Either catch him in the act or forget it! It is a waste of your and your dog's time—in his mind, you are reprimanding him for whatever he is doing at that moment.

The following behavioral problems represent some which owners most commonly encounter. Every dog is unique and every situation is unique. No author could purport for you to solve your Labrador Retriever's problem simply by reading a chapter in a book. Here we outline some basic "dogspeak" so that owners' chances of solving behavioral problems are increased. Discuss bad habits with your veterinarian and he/she can recommend a behavioral specialist to consult in

A dog's expression tells much about his temperament. In case of the Lab, his kind expression indicates an affable, even-tempered dog.

appropriate cases. Since behavioral abnormalities are the leading reason for owners' abandoning their pets, we hope that you will make a valiant effort to solve your Labrador Retriever's problem. Patience and understanding are virtues that dwell in every pet-loving household.

AGGRESSION

Aggression can be a very big problem in dogs. While a breed like the Labrador Retriever is most often thought of as a very friendly breed and a great family pet, there is no breed that is completely without aggression. Aggression, when not controlled, becomes dangerous. An aggressive dog, no matter the size, may lunge at, bite or even attack a person or another dog. Aggressive behavior is not to be tolerated. It is more than just inappropriate behavior; it is not

CAUSES OF AGGRESSION
Behavioral specialists catalog canine aggression to include not only dominant aggression and aggression with other dogs but also fear-induced, intrasexual, learned, protective (food, property, etc.), parental, pain-induced and predatory aggressions. Medical conditions can also spur aggression in dogs, including hypothyroidism, hyperthyroidism, hydrocephalus, hormonal imbalance and epilepsy.

safe. It is painful for a family to watch their dog become unpredictable in his behavior to the point where they are afraid of the dog. And while not all aggressive behavior is dangerous, it can be frightening: growling, baring teeth, etc. It is important to get to the root of the problem to ascertain why the dog is acting in this manner. Aggression is a

"Pack order" among puppies is established through roughhousing and play-fighting between littermates.

display of dominance, and the dog should not have the dominant role in its pack, which is, in this case, your family.

It is important not to challenge an aggressive dog as this could provoke an attack. Observe your Labrador Retriever's body language. Does he make direct eye contact and stare? Does he try to make himself as large as possible: ears cocked, chest out, tail erect? Height and size signify authority in a dog pack—being taller or "above" another dog literally means that he is "above" in the social status. These body signals tell you that your Labrador Retriever thinks he is in charge, a problem that needs to be dealt with. An aggressive dog is unpredictable in that you never know when he is going to strike and what he is going to do. You cannot understand why a dog that is playful and loving one minute is growling and snapping the next.

Fear is a common cause of aggression in dogs. If you can isolate what brings out the fear reaction, you can help the dog get over it. Supervise your Labrador Retriever's interactions with people and other dogs, and praise the dog when it goes well. If he starts to act aggressively in a situation, correct him and remove him from the situation. Do not let people approach the dog and start petting him without your express permission. That way, you can

have the dog sit to accept petting, and praise him when he behaves properly. You are focusing on praise and on modifying his behavior by rewarding him when he acts appropriately. By being gentle and by supervising his interactions, you are showing him that there is no need to be afraid or defensive.

The best solution is to consult a behavioral specialist, one who has experience with the Labrador Retriever specifically. Together,

SMILE!

Dogs and humans may be the only animals that smile. A dog will imitate the smile on his owner's face when he greets a friend. The dog only smiles at his human friends; he never smiles at another dog or cat. Usually, a dog rolls up his lips and shows his teeth in a clenched mouth while rolling over onto his back, begging for a soft scratch.

perhaps you can pinpoint the cause of your dog's aggression and do something about it. An aggressive dog cannot be trusted, and a dog that cannot be trusted is not safe to have as a family pet. If the pet Labrador Retriever becomes untrustworthy, he cannot be kept in the home with the family. The family must get rid of the dog. In the *very worst* case, unlikely with the Lab, the dog must be euthanized.

AGGRESSION TOWARD OTHER DOGS
A dog's aggressive behavior toward another dog stems from not enough exposure to other dogs at an early age. If other dogs make your Labrador Retriever nervous and agitated, he will lash out as a protective mechanism. A dog who has not received sufficient exposure to other canines tends to believe that he is the only dog on the planet. The animal becomes so dominant that he does not even show signs that he is fearful or threatened. Without growling or any other physical signal as a warning, he will lunge at and bite the other dog. A way to correct this is to let your Labrador Retriever approach another dog when walking on a leash. Watch very closely and at the very first sign of aggression, correct your Labrador Retriever and pull him away. Scold him for any sign of discomfort, and then praise him when he ignores or tolerates the other dog. Keep this up until either he stops the aggressive

A face-to-face meeting! Labs are friendly dogs that do well in multi-pet households.

FEAR IN A GROWN DOG

Fear in a grown dog is often the result of improper or incomplete socialization as a pup, or it can be the result of a traumatic experience he suffered when young. Keep in mind that the term "traumatic" is relative—something that you would not think twice about can leave a lasting negative impression on a puppy. If the dog experiences a similar experience later in life, he may try to fight back to protect himself. Again, this behavior is very unpredictable, especially if you do not know what is triggering his fear.

DOMINANT AGGRESSION

A social hierarchy is firmly established in a wild dog pack. The dog wants to dominate those under him and please those above him. Dogs know that there must be a leader. If you are not the obvious choice for emperor, the dog will assume the throne! These conflicting innate desires are what a dog owner is up against when he sets about training a dog. In training a dog to obey commands, the owner is reinforcing that he is the top dog in the "pack" and that the dog should, and should want to, serve his superior. Thus, the owner is suppressing the dog's urge to dominate by modifying his behavior and making him obedient.

behavior, learns to ignore the other dog or even accepts other dogs. Praise him lavishly for his correct behavior.

A typical Lab will welcome the friendship of all! This Lab and his Rottweiler buddy share some quiet time.

An important part of training is taking every opportunity to reinforce that you are the leader. The simple action of making your Labrador Retriever sit to wait for his food instead of allowing him to run up to get it when he wants it says that you control when he eats; he is dependent on you for food. Although it may be difficult, do not give in to your dog's wishes every time he whines at you or looks at you with pleading eyes. It is a constant effort to show the dog that his place in the pack is at the bottom. This is not meant to sound cruel or inhumane. You love your Labrador Retriever and you should treat him with care and affection. You (hopefully) did not get a dog just so you could boss around another creature. Dog training is not about being cruel or feeling important, it is about molding the dog's behavior into what is acceptable and teaching him to live by your rules. In theory, it is quite simple: catch him in appropriate behavior and reward him for it. Add a dog into the equation and it becomes a bit more trying, but as a rule of thumb, positive reinforcement is what works best.

With a dominant dog, punishment and negative reinforcement can have the opposite effect of what you are after. It can make a dog fearful and/or act out aggressively if he feels he is being challenged. Remember, a dominant dog perceives himself at the top of the social heap, and will fight to defend his perceived status. The best way to prevent that is to never give him reason to think that he is in control in the first place. If you are having trouble training your Labrador Retriever and it seems as if he is constantly challenging your authority, seek the help of an obedience trainer or behavioral specialist. A professional will work with both you and your dog to teach you effective techniques to use at home. Beware of trainers who rely on excessively harsh methods; scolding is necessary

THE MIGHTY MALE

Males, whether castrated or not, will mount almost anything: a pillow, your leg or, much to your dismay, even your neighbor's leg. As with other types of inappropriate behavior, the dog must be corrected while in the act, which for once is not difficult. Often he will not let go! While a puppy is experimenting with his very first urges, his owners feel he needs to "sow his oats" and allow the pup to mount. As the pup grows into a full-size dog, with full-size urges, it becomes a nuisance and an embarrassment. Males always appear as if they are trying to "save the race," more determined and stronger than imaginable. While altering the dog at an appropriate age will limit the dog's desire, it usually does not remove it entirely.

now and then, but the focus in your training should *always* be on positive reinforcement.

SEXUAL BEHAVIOR

Dogs exhibit certain sexual behaviors that may have influenced your choice of male or female when you first purchased your Labrador Retriever. Spaying and neutering will eliminate these behaviors, but if you are purchasing a dog that you wish to breed, you should be aware of what you will have to deal with throughout the dog's life.

Female dogs usually have two estruses per year, each season lasting about three weeks. These are the only times in which a female dog will mate, and she usually will not allow this until the second week of the cycle. If a bitch is not bred during the heat cycle, it is not uncommon for her to experience a false pregnancy, in which her mammary glands swell and she exhibits maternal tendencies toward toys or other objects.

Owners must further recognize that mounting is not merely a sexual expression but also one of dominance, seen in males and females alike. Be consistent and persistent in discouraging this behavior and you will find that you can move "mounters."

CHEWING

The national canine pastime is chewing! Every dog loves to sink

A young friend and something to chew mean a content Lab puppy!

his "canines" into a tasty bone, but most anything will do! Dogs need to chew, to massage their gums, to make their new teeth feel better and to exercise their jaws. This is a natural behavior deeply imbedded in all things canine. Our role as owners is not to stop chewing, but to redirect it to positive, chew-worthy objects. Be an informed owner and purchase proper chew toys for your Labrador Retriever, like strong nylon bones made for large dogs. Be sure that the devices are safe and durable, since your dog's safety is at risk. Again, the owner is responsible for ensuring a dog-proof environment. The best answer is prevention: that is, put your shoes, handbags and other tasty objects in their proper places (out of the reach of the growing canine mouth). Direct puppies to their toys whenever you see them tasting the furniture legs or the leg of your pants. Make a loud noise to attract the pup's attention and immediately escort him to his chew toy and engage him with the toy for at least four minutes, praising and encouraging him all the while.

Some trainers recommend deterrents, such as hot pepper or another bitter spice or a product designed for this purpose, to discourage the dog from chewing on unwanted objects. This is sometimes reliable, though not as often as the manufacturers of such products claim. Test out the product with your own dog before investing in a case of it.

JUMPING UP
Jumping up is a dog's friendly way of saying hello! Some dog owners do not mind when their dog jumps up, which is fine for them. The problem arises when guests come

Your Lab will usually be so excited to see you that he won't be able to keep all fours on the ground!

to the house and the dog greets them in the same manner— whether they like it or not! However friendly the greeting may be, chances are your visitors will not appreciate nearly being knocked over by 60 or more pounds of Labrador Retriever. The dog will not be able to distinguish upon whom he can jump and whom he cannot. Therefore, it is probably best to discourage this behavior entirely.

Pick a command such as "Off" (avoid using "Down" since you will use that for the dog to lie down) and tell him "Off" when he jumps up. Place him on the ground on all fours and have him sit, praising him the whole time. Always lavish him with praise and petting when he is in the "sit" position. That way you are still giving him a warm affectionate greeting, because you are as excited to see him as he is to see you!

DIGGING
Digging, which is seen as a destructive behavior to humans, is actually quite a natural behavior in dogs. Even though your Lab is not one of the "earth dogs" (also known as terriers), his desire to dig can be irrepressible and most frustrating to his owners. When digging occurs in your yard, it is actually a normal behavior redirected into something the dog can do in his everyday life. For example, in the wild a dog would be actively seeking food,

making his own shelter, etc. He would be using his paws in a purposeful manner; he would be using them for his survival. Since you provide him with food and shelter, he has no need to use his paws for these purposes, and so the energy that he would be using manifests itself in the form of little holes all over your yard and flower gardens.

Perhaps your dog is digging as a reaction to boredom—it is somewhat similar to someone eating a whole bag of chips in front of the television—because they are there and there is not anything better to do! Basically, the answer is to provide the dog with adequate play and exercise so that his mind and paws are occupied, and so that he feels as if he is doing something useful.

Of course, digging is easiest to control if it is stopped as soon as possible, but it is often hard to catch a dog in the act, especially if he is alone in the garden during the day. If your dog is a compulsive digger and is not easily distracted by other activities, you can designate an area on your property where it is okay for him to dig. If you catch him digging in an off-limits area of the yard, immediately bring him to the approved area and praise him for digging there. Keep a close eye on him so that you can catch him; that is the only way he is going to understand what is permitted and what is not. If you

Your alert Lab will be very aware of what's going on in and around "his" property, and will likely use his voice to give you a report.

bring him to a hole he dug an hour ago and tell him "no," he will understand that you are not fond of holes, or dirt, or flowers. If you catch him while he is stifle-deep in your tulips, that is when he will get your message.

BARKING

Dogs cannot talk—oh, what they would say if they could! Instead, barking is a dog's way of "talking." It can be somewhat frustrating because it is not always easy to tell what a dog means by his bark—is he excited, happy, frightened, angry? Whatever it is that the dog is trying to say, he should not be punished for barking. It is only when the barking becomes excessive, and when the excessive barking becomes a bad habit, does the behavior need to be modified.

If an intruder came into your home in the middle of the night and the dog barked a warning, wouldn't you be pleased? You would probably deem your dog a hero, a wonderful guardian and protector of the home. On the other hand, if a friend drops by unexpectedly and rings the doorbell and is greeted with a sudden sharp bark, you would probably be annoyed at the dog. But isn't it just the same behavior? The dog does not know any better…unless he sees who is at the door and it is someone he is familiar with, he will bark as a means of vocalizing that his (and your) territory is being threatened. While your friend is not posing a threat, it is all the same to the dog. Barking is his means of letting you know that there is an intrusion, whether friend or foe, on your property. This type of barking is instinctive and should not be discouraged.

Excessive habitual barking, however, is a problem that should be corrected early on. As your Labrador Retriever grows up, you will be able to tell when his barking is purposeful and when it is for no reason. You will become able to distinguish your dog's different barks and with what they are associated. For example, the bark when someone comes to the door will be different from the bark when he is excited to see you. It is similar to a person's tone of voice, except that the dog has to rely totally on tone of voice because he does not have the benefit of using words. An incessant barker will be evident at an early age.

There are some things that encourage a dog to bark. For example, if your dog barks non-stop for a few minutes and you give him a treat to quiet him, he believes that you are rewarding him for barking. He will associate barking with getting a treat, and will keep doing it until he is rewarded.

FOOD STEALING

Is your dog devising ways of stealing food from your counter-tops? If so, you must answer the following questions: Is your Labrador Retriever hungry, or is he "constantly famished" like every other chow hound? Why is there food on the countertop?

TRAINING TIP

To encourage proper barking, you can teach your dog the command "Quiet." When someone comes to the door and the dog barks a few times, praise him. Talk to him soothingly and, when he stops barking, tell him "Quiet" and continue to praise him. In this sense, you are letting him bark his warning, which is an instinctive behavior, and then rewarding him for being quiet after a few barks. You may initially reward him with a treat after he has been quiet for a few minutes.

Face it, some dogs are more food-motivated than others; some dogs are totally obsessed by a slab of brisket and can only think of their next meal. Food stealing is terrific fun and always yields a great reward—*food*, glorious food!

The owner's goal, therefore, is to make the "reward" less rewarding, even startling! Plant a shaker can (an empty pop can with coins inside) on the counter so that it catches your pooch off-guard. There are other devices available that will surprise the dog when he is looking for a mid-afternoon snack. Such remote-control devices, though not the first choice of some trainers, allow the correction to come from the object instead of the owner. These devices are also useful to keep the snacking hound from napping on furniture that is forbidden.

BEGGING

Just like food stealing, begging is a favorite pastime of hungry puppies! With that same reward—*food*! Dogs quickly learn that their owners keep the "good food" for themselves, and that we humans do not dine on kibble alone. Begging is a conditioned response related to a specific stimulus, time and place. The sounds of the kitchen, cans and bottles opening, crinkling bags, the smell of food in preparation, etc., will excite the chow hound and soon the paws are in the air!

Here is the solution to stopping this behavior: Never give into a beggar! You are rewarding the dog for sitting pretty, jumping up, whining and rubbing his nose into you by giving him that glorious reward—*food*. By ignoring the dog, you will (eventually) force the behavior into extinction. Note that the behavior likely gets worse before it disappears, so be sure there are not any "softies" in the family who will give in to little "Oliver" every time he whimpers, "More, please."

SEPARATION ANXIETY

Your Labrador Retriever may howl, whine or otherwise vocalize his displeasure at your leaving the house and his being left alone. This is a normal case of separa-

Your Lab needs to know that *his* food comes from *his* bowl, not from your countertop or dinner plate.

tion anxiety, but there are things that can be done to eliminate this problem. Your dog needs to learn that he will be fine on his own for a while and that he will not wither away if he is not attended to every minute of the day. In fact, constant attention can lead to separation anxiety in the first place. If you are endlessly coddling and cuddling your dog, he will come to expect this from you all of the time and it will be more traumatic for him when you are not there.

Obviously, you enjoy spending time with your dog, and he thrives on your love and attention. However, it should not become a dependent relationship where he is heartbroken without you. One thing you can do to minimize separation anxiety is to make your entrances and exits as low-key as possible. Do not give your dog a long drawn-out goodbye, and do not lavish him with hugs and kisses when you return. This is giving in to the attention that he craves, and it will only make him miss it more when you are away. Another thing you can try is to give your dog a treat when you leave; this will not only keep him occupied and keep his mind off the fact that you just left, but it will also help him associate your leaving with a pleasant experience.

You may have to accustom your dog to being left alone in intervals, much like when you introduced your pup to his crate. Of course, when your dog starts whimpering as you approach the door, your first instinct will be to run to him and comfort him, but do not do it! Eventually he will adjust and be just fine if you take it in small steps. His anxiety stems from being placed in an unfamiliar situation; by familiarizing him with being alone he will learn that he is okay. That is not to say you should purposely leave your dog home alone, but the dog needs to know that while he can depend on you for his care, you do not have to be by his side 24 hours a day.

When the dog is alone in the house, he should be confined to his crate or a designated dog-proof area of the house. This should be the area in which he sleeps, so he should already feel comfortable there and this should make him feel more at ease when he is alone. This is just one of the many examples in which a crate is an invaluable tool for you and your dog, and another reinforcement of why your dog should view his crate as a "happy" place, a place of his own.

COPROPHAGIA
Feces eating is, to most humans, one of the most disgusting behaviors that their dog could engage in, yet to the dog it is perfectly normal. It is hard for us

to understand why a dog would want to eat its own feces—he could be seeking certain nutrients that are missing from his diet, he could be just plain hungry or he could be attracted by the pleasing (to a dog) scent. While copro-phagia most often refers to the dog eating his own feces, a dog may likely eat that of another animal as well if he comes across it. Dogs often find the stool of cats and horses more palatable than that of other dogs.

Vets have found that diets with a low digestibility, containing relatively low levels of fiber and high levels of starch, increase coprophagia. Therefore, high-fiber diets may decrease the likelihood of dogs' eating feces. Both the consistency of the stool (how firm it feels in the dog's mouth) and the presence of undigested nutrients increase the likelihood. Once the dog develops diarrhea from feces eating, it will likely quit this distasteful habit, since dogs tend to prefer eating harder feces.

To discourage this behavior, first make sure that the food you are feeding your dog is nutrition-ally complete and that he is getting enough food. If changes in his diet do not seem to work, and no medical cause can be found, you will have to modify the behavior through environmental control before it becomes a habit. There are some tricks you can try,

"LONELY WOLF"
The number of dogs that suffer from separation anxiety is on the rise as more and more pet owners find themselves at work all day. New attention is being paid to this problem, which is especially hard to diagnose since it is only evident when the dog is alone. Research is currently being done to help educate dog owners about separation anxiety and how they can help minimize this problem in their dogs.

such as adding an unpleasant-tasting substance to the feces to make them unpalatable or adding something to the dog's food which will make it unpleasant tasting after it passes through the dog. The best way to prevent your dog from eating his stool is to make it unavailable—clean up after he eliminates and remove any stool from the yard. If it is not there, he cannot eat it.

Never reprimand the dog for stool eating, as this rarely impresses the dog. Vets recommend distracting the dog while he is in the act of stool eating. Another option is to muzzle the dog when he is in the garden to relieve himself; this usually is effective within 30 to 60 days. Coprophagia most frequently is seen in pups 6 to 12 months of age, and usually disappears around the dog's first birthday.

My Labrador Retriever

PUT YOUR PUPPY'S FIRST PICTURE HERE

Dog's Name _____

Date _____ Photographer _____